OCR GCSE

Business Studies

Neil Denby

Philip Allan, an imprint of Hodder Education, an Hachette UK company,
Blenheim Court, George Street, Banbury, Oxfordshire OX16 5BH

Orders
Bookpoint Ltd, 130 Milton Park, Abingdon, Oxfordshire OX14 4SB
tel: 01235 827827
fax: 01235 400401
e-mail: education@bookpoint.co.uk
Lines are open 9.00 a.m.–5.00 p.m., Monday to Saturday, with a 24-hour message answering
service. You can also order through the Philip Allan Updates website: www.philipallan.co.uk

Copyright © 2010 Neil Denby
ISBN 978-1-4441-0778-4

First printed 2010
Impression number   8
Year   2015

Printed in Dubai

Hachette UK's policy is to use papers that are natural, renewable and recyclable products and
made from wood grown in sustainable forests. The logging and manufacturing processes are
expected to conform to the environmental regulations of the country of origin.

P02100

Contents

Introduction

How to revise

Revision is not just about remembering, but about being able to apply what you have remembered to business situations. You should, therefore, make sure that you do not just learn facts, but know how a business would use them in its decision making. There are very few questions that will ask you for straightforward knowledge.

10 tips for effective revision

1 Start revising in plenty of time. You may have to revisit some topics at the last minute, but you should try to make sure there are only a few of these.
2 Have a set time and place, where you cannot be disturbed, for your revision sessions.
3 Plan revision carefully — make sure you leave enough time to cover everything.
4 Plan short-term targets — 'I will have learnt *xxx* by *xxx*.' These show you are making progress and help to motivate you.
5 Do not do too much! Your brain needs regular rests in order to be able to process and store information properly.
6 Revise topics three times. This will help to put the knowledge into your long-term memory.
7 Make sure your revision is active — make notes, use spider diagrams, pictograms and mind maps, write raps or lyrics. Sound and visual reminders are usually better than just words.
8 Think about using new technology. You could make a podcast of a revision topic and listen to it on your MP3 player.
9 Practise applying your knowledge to business situations. Use the questions in this book to practise your examination technique. Make sure you draw on all the relevant information, not just a single topic.
10 Revise with someone else — then you can test each other, compare notes, etc.

How to use this book

Each chapter in the book is short and contains the basic knowledge you will need to pass at GCSE. In each topic there are a number of features.

■ *What the specification requires.* This tells you the sort of knowledge that the specification needs you to know, and steers you in the direction of the types of question that can be asked.

- *In brief.* This states the knowledge requirement in a couple of sentences. For last-minute refreshers, this is what you will need.

- *Revision notes.* This feature outlines the area of knowledge that it is absolutely essential for you to know about each topic.

- *Speak the language.* This gives the key terms and definitions that you will need for a particular topic. In all GCSE business examinations, there are marks for using the correct technical language. These are highlighted in the text.

- *In a nutshell.* This contains the key points from the topic as a bullet list.

- *Boost your grade.* This feature tells you how to access AO1 knowledge marks or how to move from AO1 to AO2 explanation and context marks or from AO2 to AO3 analysis, recommendation and judgement marks.

- *Test yourself.* This provides a short test on the content of all or part of the topic. It takes the form of multiple-choice questions, missing-word questions or tests that you can self-set.

At the end of each section, you will find a longer question, a set of multiple-choice questions or a similar exercise to test your knowledge. At the end of each unit, you will find a full practice examination paper, just like the one that you will sit for your GCSE.

Suggested answers to all the questions are available online at:
www.hodderplus.co.uk/philipallan.

OCR GCSE Business Studies

The OCR GCSE Business Studies qualification is based on the two previous OCR specifications but has been revised and updated to take account of new Business Studies subject criteria. It is a single-award GCSE. There are other routes within the OCR 'suite' of business qualifications, such as Leisure and Tourism and Applied Business which provide for double-award and short-course qualifications.

The route to this GCSE qualification is through the two examined units:
Unit A292 Business and people
Unit A293 Production, finance and the external business environment

plus the controlled assessment unit:
Unit A291 Marketing and enterprise

The specification also acts as a springboard for further study at AS or A-level. This book covers all three units in equal depth because if you are to succeed in the controlled assessment task, you must have good knowledge of the content of this unit.

Unit A292 Business and people

This is a compulsory unit, which is examined with a single 1-hour paper, consisting mostly of short-answer and data-response questions. The paper is marked out of 60 and tests mainly knowledge and application. Remember that papers will not cover the whole of the content, but will choose to concentrate on different content each year. The paper has some items and diagrams for you to use.

The unit contains four sections:
- Business activity
- Business ownership and location
- The workforce in business
- Business organisation

Business activity
This section covers why business activity takes place and some of the people involved. Stakeholders are the people (like you) who have a stake in businesses. What stakeholders want will also affect business aims and objectives.

Business ownership and location
This section covers the ways in which both small and large businesses may be legally established and the benefits and drawbacks of these different types of legal structure. It looks at large and public sector businesses and how businesses become large. The various factors that affect location are also considered.

The workforce in business
All businesses need someone to work for them, even if it is only the owner. Where there are employees, these must be recruited and paid, trained and motivated. This section also covers the restrictions laid on business by government legislation and how businesses deal with industrial relations.

Business organisation
This section covers internal organisation structures, and the relationships and communications within them, as well as the functional areas into which a business can be divided. It looks at how businesses can change and the effects of this on the workforce.

A293 Production, finance and the external business environment
This is a compulsory unit that is examined with a single 90-minute paper. The paper consists of short-answer and data-response type questions to test your knowledge and application, and more detailed questions to test your skills of analysis and evaluation.

The questions are based on a case study, consisting of a number of documents relating to a business. This material is released to candidates over 8 weeks before the examination. You can use it to guess what might be covered. Remember, though, that the examiners can ask questions on any part of the specification, so you should make sure you have learned all the relevant areas.

The unit contains four sections:
- Using and managing resources
- Financial information and decision making
- Business issues and influences
- The wider world

Using and managing resources

This section covers the production side of business. It looks at methods of production, how businesses can add value to production and the maintenance of quality. It looks at how businesses cost production and the benefits they can gain from growing larger.

Financial information and decision making

This section covers how businesses can raise the finance with which they start and further sources of finance that will help them expand and grow once established. It looks at some of the forecasts and calculations undertaken by businesses to determine their cash-flow position and possible problems and profitability.

Business issues and influences

This section considers some of the major factors which affect the behaviour and reputation of businesses, such as environmental and ethical issues. It also looks at market structures and how all businesses can be affected by the ups and downs of the business cycle.

The wider world

There are many influences on business that are outside the control of the business, both at home and abroad. These include government and EU policies and the effect of changes in interest rates and currency exchange rates.

How is my work marked?

You will be marked on your knowledge, application and higher skills such as analysis and evaluation.

- Assessment Objective 1 (AO1) is for knowledge and understanding, including the correct use of business terms.
- Assessment Objective 2 (AO2) is for applying your knowledge and understanding to a situation. It usually means answering a question in context — that is, using the business given. Your examples should therefore always be appropriate to the business that you are given.
- Assessment Objective 3 (AO3) is for analysis and evaluation. Analysis is weighing up the advantages and disadvantages, or the benefits and drawbacks, of a situation. Evaluation is making judgements, making recommendations and drawing conclusions supported by your knowledge or the data you are given.

Unit A291 Marketing and enterprise

Unit A291 is the controlled assessment unit, which is based on the marketing section of the specification.

Controlled assessment is a new type of assessment that is replacing coursework. It tests the same sort of skills as coursework used to test, but under conditions that are more controlled. Controlled assessments are designed to be:

- researched independently
- completed during lessons within a set time
- supervised during the final write-up

This means that, with most assessments, you can undertake the research at home, or in a library, or on the internet. You can then use this research to help you with your final write-up. You can take a folder or portfolio of your research into the classroom when you are doing your final write-up.

Your teacher can give you feedback on your focus and on the sort of research that you are undertaking. This must all take place before the final write-up. The final stage is a supervised period to write up your research findings. This can be spread across a number of sessions.

For the OCR controlled assessment, you will be given some background information on a business. This will be written information, charts and graphs, and numerical data.

You will be required to carry out three investigations:
- Investigation 1 uses the data provided and is marked out of 10. Really, this is a practice investigation.
- Investigation 2 requires you to collect your own data and is marked out of 25.
- Investigation 3 requires you to collect your own data and is marked out of 25.
- You will be marked on three skills:
  - your ability to select relevant information and to use your own knowledge and understanding
  - the way in which you apply that knowledge to an issue, using the data
  - the way in which you analyse the information in order to reach a judgement or recommendation.

Unit A292
Business and people

Business activity

Topic 1

The need for business activity

What the specification requires

You will need to know about why businesses exist to fulfil consumer wants. Consumers want goods and services; businesses supply them. You should understand that they do this in competition with other businesses, for various different reasons, only one of which is **profit**.

In brief

A market is anywhere that a buyer and seller come together to agree on a sale. The business that is doing the selling needs to know as much as possible about the customer who is doing the buying in order to succeed. Most businesses succeed by either finding or creating a **gap in the market** — by offering a product that is wanted, but which other businesses do not provide. If they are successful, they will attract competitors to that market.

Just one sort of market — with products, demand and supply

Revision notes

- Making sure that the business knows what customers want, and then providing it, is essential to success. By providing **products** to the customers who want them, businesses are operating in a market.
- A market is anywhere that buyers and sellers come together to agree on the price for an amount of a product. This does not have to be a physical place: markets can take place via telephone or online.

A product will be either a **good** or a **service**. Goods are things that can be touched; services are done for or to a customer. Businesses will target particular parts of a market, called segments. Segments can be more easily targeted. Common ways to segment a market are by age, geography, gender, hobbies and interests, and socioeconomic group — that is, the level of income and education enjoyed by a household.

- New businesses look for a gap in the market. A gap in the market is where a demand exists, but it is not being met. Businesses can map their market by listing its key features, then seeing where there are gaps. Businesses can find out about the wants of customers through market research. Some businesses are able to create a gap in the market by, for example, offering a completely new type of product.

- If a business successfully sells a product in a market, this will attract competition. All businesses operate in competitive markets, so they will seek ways to compete more effectively. As businesses succeed or fail in this, markets are constantly changing and businesses need to adapt to that change.

In a nutshell

* Businesses provide products to markets.
* To succeed, they need to find a gap in the market.
* This means analysing the market — both buyers and sellers.
* This can be achieved through market research.
* Businesses that succeed attract competitors.
* Competition in a market is constantly changing.

Speak the language

profit — the surplus of income (revenue) over costs

gap in the market — where there is demand, but no product to fill it

products — goods and services

goods — those things that can be touched

services — those things done to or for a customer

Test yourself

Fill in the missing words using the list below. If you are feeling confident, cover the words and do the exercise from memory.

Businesses are set up in order to provide the .... that people need and want. Businesses sell and customers buy. This is called a .... Goods are things that can be touched as opposed to things done for or to a customer, called .... Markets are often divided into .... These can then be more easily targeted. Common ways of .... include age, geography, gender , hobbies and interests, and ....: that is, the level of income and education enjoyed by a household. If a business is successful, this will attract .... All businesses operate in .... that are constantly changing.

competition   competitive markets   market   products

segmentation   segments   services   socioeconomic group

Boost your grade

AO1: to access Level 1 marks you need to understand that the most important part of a business transaction is usually the customer. Being able to explain that keeping the customer happy is the basis for business success will give you AO1 marks.

The influence of stakeholders

What the specification requires

You need to know what is meant by the term **stakeholder** in connection with business. You should be able to identify the main stakeholders in a business, and comment on their interest in the business, their influence on it, and how this might conflict with other stakeholders' interests.

In brief

Businesses can only exist if people take risks on new products or ideas or in new markets. The owners of the business are usually the ones who carry most of the risk. They obviously have a stake in how well the business succeeds. Once a business does exist, there will be many people, other than the owners, who will have an interest in its success (or failure). Stakeholders are those people, groups or organisations that have a stake in a business.

Employees are internal stakeholders

Revision notes

- Stakeholders with a direct interest in the business are called **internal stakeholders** and include owners and employees. In a small business, the owner(s) will be a single person (sole trader), or a small group of people (partnerships, co-operatives, private limited companies).
- **Shareholders** are a special group of owners. Each has a share of the business. In private limited companies, shareholders are limited to family and friends.
- Owners would like success and profit. They can influence a business by investing. Owners make key decisions about the business, such as what to sell, what markets to operate in and whether to expand.
- Employees would like decent working conditions and fair pay. Employees can influence the business through working hard and being skilled and motivated, or by failing in these.
- Managers are the employees who help run the business. Their influence extends to taking day-to-day decisions in the business.
- **External stakeholders** have a less direct stake in a business. They include customers, suppliers, banks, communities, government and pressure groups.

- Customers want quality and reliability. They influence the business by buying or not. Suppliers influence the business through quality and reliability of supply.
- Financial stakeholders, such as banks, have lent or given the business money. They can take decisions that are in their own interests, rather than those of the business. Sometimes stakeholder groups have conflicting aims.
- The community may want the business for some reasons (e.g. employment) but not others (e.g. pollution). Government influences business through laws and taxation. Pressure groups are groups of people set up to bring about change. They try to influence businesses to make the changes they want.

In a nutshell

* All businesses have stakeholders.
* Internal stakeholders have a direct stake.
* They can influence the business through the way they work and make decisions.
* External stakeholders have a more indirect stake.
* They can have a lot of influence on a small business (e.g. customers not buying, suppliers not supplying quality, governments setting tax too high).
* Sometimes stakeholder aims conflict.

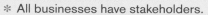

Test yourself

Try this exam-style question.

Angie owns a drive-in burger bar. It normally shuts at 10 p.m. As the local cinema has decided to stay open until midnight, Angie has decided to extend her opening hours. She is in a residential district and local people have complained about late-night traffic noise. They have appealed to the local council to restrict the burger bar to 10 p.m. closing.

1 Identify two stakeholders in this situation. *(2 marks)*

2 Select two stakeholders and explain how their aims conflict. *(3 marks)*

3 Advise the council whether or not to uphold the appeal. *(7 marks)*

Boost your grade

AO2 to AO3: AO3 marks will be indicated by the key words 'analyse' or 'evaluate'. This means you must look at both sides of an argument with equal weight. You may then be asked to make a decision (e.g. between the conflicting aims of two groups of stakeholders). There is no right or wrong answer. AO3 marks are gained for the reasons you give for your judgement.

Business aims and objectives

What the specification requires

You need to know and understand the difference between **aims** and **objectives** and why a business sets them for itself. You should know the main types of objective, such as survival, profit, growth, and personal objectives such as job satisfaction or providing a service. You should understand how and why these might be different according to the type of business activity. You should know how objectives are used to help measure success.

In brief

Businesses need to know whether or not they are making progress or succeeding in what they are trying to do. To find this out, they need to measure their progress. Progress can be measured by using aims and objectives. Aims are long term and shape how the business operates. Objectives are shorter term and can be used to help run the business. Progress can be measured by setting and reaching objectives.

Revision notes

- Aims are long-term goals towards which the business can work. They are often not precise; a business may, for instance, aim to be 'the customer's first choice', 'the best in the world' or 'always out in front'. Sometimes the aim of a business will be contained in its **mission statement** or vision. Most businesses aim to satisfy their customers.
- The steps on the way to achieving an aim will be marked by shorter-term objectives. These will be more clearly defined than aims — setting them helps the business move forward. Progress can be measured by seeing how well objectives have been met. SMART is the term used to remember what objectives should be to be useful to a business. SMART objectives are Specific, Measurable, Achievable, Realistic and Time-related.
- The main objective for a start-up business is survival; further objectives may be profit, growth or bigger market share. Owners may also want to achieve other aims, such as independence, a good reputation, providing a local service and having loyal customers.
- Small businesses are likely to have more modest objectives than larger ones. Many small business objectives will be personal to the owner, such as quality of life or quality of service.

A football club can measure its progress by its position in the league

■ The different objectives of stakeholders may sometimes conflict. Objectives may also need to change over time as the business changes. Once an objective is achieved, a new one may be set. For example, once profitability is achieved, a business may look for a certain level of profit.

In a nutshell

* Aims are long-term 'wishes'.
* Objectives are shorter-term and more precise.
* The main objective of a start-up business will be survival.
* Further objectives include profit, growth and bigger market share.
* Objectives may change as the business changes or as they are achieved.
* Sometimes different groups that influence a business will have conflicting objectives.
* Objectives can be used to help manage a business and measure its progress.

Test yourself

Try this exam-style question.

Rachel has started a business called Kidzstuff, selling children's clothes. She designs and makes the clothes herself. She has decided to rent a shop in her village for 6 months to build up trade.

1 Identify a suitable long-term objective for Kidzstuff. *(1 mark)*

2 Explain why this is a relevant aim for Rachel's business. *(2 marks)*

3 Explain how Rachel could use short-term objectives to help achieve the long-term one. *(2 marks)*

Boost your grade

AO1 to AO2: to reach AO2 marks you may need to explain the difference between aims and objectives. You may need to give relevant examples from the business in the question paper. Always put your answer in the context of this business.

Topic 4

Social enterprises

What the specification requires

You will need to understand that not all businesses have similar objectives. Some, called social enterprises, will have objectives that are meant to benefit a group of their members, customers or employees, or even the communities in which they work. Questions may ask about the ethical and moral reasons for social enterprises and why their objectives may be different from those of other businesses.

In brief

Most businesses will try to make a profit. This is so that their owners can share in the success of the business. In some special cases, businesses do not work to make a profit. They have other, social, objectives, and so are called **social enterprises**. Social objectives bring benefits to particular stakeholder groups such as communities, employees and customers. There are often ethical and moral reasons for social enterprises, rooted in the business being fair and not exploiting suppliers, workers, customers or other stakeholders. Being 'ethical' means doing the right, or moral, thing.

Revision notes

- Social enterprises include co-operatives, mutual societies, charities and voluntary groups.
- **Co-operatives** and **mutual societies** want to make sure that their members (customers and employees) get a fair deal. When a cooperative is established, each member puts in the same amount of money. Each shares equally in the control of the business and takes an equal share of profits. In larger co-operatives, management control may fall to a smaller group, but these will be elected by all the membership. The main types of co-operative are as follows:
  - Worker co-operatives — a group of workers pool their labour to produce a good or service.
  - Producer co-operatives — a group of producers share costs and help each other to sell what they produce. These co-operatives are often agricultural and share expensive machinery which each needs for only a short time. They can also get better prices if they all agree on similar prices.
  - Consumer co-operatives — these are generally retail organisations that buy products on behalf of members and make sure that they are sold at fair prices.
- A mutual society is also a type of co-operative. They were set up to provide members with financial help. Originally they were insurance societies protecting against fire or theft, building societies (to help members buy houses) and even funeral societies (to pay for funerals and provide pensions). Many have now grown into big businesses and have become household names.

Farmers in a co-operative may share one machine

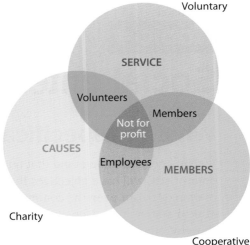

- **Charities** want to maximise the amount of good that they can do, which usually means raising as much money as possible for their particular cause.
- Voluntary groups usually provide a service to the community. People volunteer to work for them. Examples are St John Ambulance and the Royal National Lifeboat Institution. These groups may also be supported by charitable donations.

In a nutshell

- Social enterprises include co-operatives, mutual societies, charities and voluntary groups.
- Co-operatives and mutual societies want to make sure that their members (customers and employees) get a fair deal.
- The main types of co-operative are worker co-operatives, producer co-operatives and consumer co-operatives.
- A mutual society is also a type of co-operative. They were set up to provide members with financial help.
- Charities want to maximise the amount of good that they can do, which usually means raising as much money as possible for their particular cause.
- Voluntary groups usually provide a service to the community.

Test yourself

Choose the most appropriate answer from each of following alternatives.

1 Which of the following do members of a co-operative share equally: (1) profits, (2) decision making and control (3) risk? **(a)** 1 and 2 only, **(b)** 1 and 3 only, **(c)** 2 and 3 only, **(d)** all of these, **(e)** none of these.

2 Which of the following is not a type of co-operative? **(a)** Worker, **(b)** consumer, **(c)** producer, **(d)** mutual, **(e)** company.

3 The Royal National Lifeboat Institution in the UK is an example of **(a)** a volunteer group, **(b)** a voluntary group, **(c)** a supermarket chain, **(d)** a discount club, **(e)** a cooperative.

4 A mutual society is set up to provide benefits to its **(a)** shareholders, **(b)** customers, **(c)** suppliers, **(d)** members, **(e)** workers.

5 Charities are set up to maximise **(a)** profits for a cause, **(b)** revenue for a cause, **(c)** good for a cause, **(d)** market share for a cause, **(e)** publicity for themselves.

Boost your grade

AO2 to AO3: demutualisation is still a current topic. Demutualisation is when a mutual society, in which members all have an equal say, becomes a limited company. Members have to vote for this process and many do, because they are offered shares in the new company. For AO3 marks you should be able to argue which is better: staying mutual, or becoming a company and rewarding members with shares.

Primary, secondary and tertiary sectors

What the specification requires

You will need to understand how businesses are classified into primary, secondary and tertiary sectors, and to be able to give examples to support your understanding. You will need to know about how the sectors are changing in the UK and the effect this might have on different businesses.

In brief

A good will go through several stages in its journey from raw materials to final consumer. Businesses are divided into sectors according to the stage of the production process in which they are involved. There are normally three stages of production, involving: raw materials; processing, refining or manufacturing; and distribution and retailing.

Raw materials have to be extracted or otherwise obtained by businesses in the primary sector, and factories and plant are needed for manufacturing and processing in the secondary sector. The tertiary sector contains all those services such as distribution, retail, banking, communications and insurance.

Revision notes

- The first stage of the production process is called **primary production**. Businesses in this sector are involved with raw materials. This sector includes fishing, farming and forestry as well as mining, quarrying and drilling. It includes any business which takes a material in its natural state and turns it into a 'resource' that can be used in the production process.
- The second stage of the production process is called **secondary production**. Businesses in this sector are involved with taking the raw materials or component parts and turning them into finished or part-finished goods. It therefore involves procedures such as refining, processing and manufacturing.

Ingram

Oil extraction is an example of primary production

- The third stage of the process is called **tertiary production**. Businesses in this sector are service providers. Services are needed not just in the final stage but throughout the **chain of production** to support primary and secondary industry. Insurance, banking, communications and other support services are all part of the tertiary sector (along with direct services such as transport and retailing).

- The stage of development that a country has reached is sometimes stated in terms of its main types of industry. The UK is considered to be a 'developed' economy. It has a very large service sector, a shrinking manufacturing (secondary) sector and a relatively small primary sector. This could be a problem as the UK has to rely on importing raw materials and even energy. It is not a problem as long as the service sector is earning enough money to pay for it.

Speak the language

primary production — the first stage of the production process, dealing with raw materials

secondary production — the second stage of production, dealing with making the good

tertiary production — the third stage of production, dealing with services

chain of production — the stages of production through which a product passes, from primary to secondary to tertiary

In a nutshell

* Primary production is the first stage of the production process.
* It is concerned with raw materials.
* Secondary production is the second stage of production.
* It is concerned with manufacturing and processing.
* Tertiary production is the third stage of the production process.
* It is concerned with the provision of services.

Test yourself

Try this exam-style question.

Merrion's Garage Services Ltd is a private limited company owned by John Merrion and his family. Merrion's is part of the tertiary sector of the economy.

1 Explain the term 'tertiary sector' and give another example of a business in this sector. *(2 marks)*

2 John Merrion says that tertiary sector businesses must 'stay close to their customers'. Explain:
   (a) what you think John means *(2 marks)*
   (b) how businesses like Merrion's can achieve this *(6 marks)*

Boost your grade

AO1 to AO2: for AO2 marks you must be able to put your knowledge into context. Here, for example, you should be able to give examples of businesses in each sector, such as Shell for oil extraction, Volkswagen for car manufacturing and HSBC for banking.

Section test: Business activity

Read the passage and answer the questions.

Rupert and Peter have discovered that many people do not bother to print photographs any more, but store them electronically. They found that with their own photographs they could not remember what was in a particular file, as photographs were not named. The easiest way to remember where photographs were was to print off a single sheet of thumbnails of the photographs. The friends think they have found a gap in the market.

They have decided to set up a business called Klikfit that provides thumbnails on a card that is the right size to fit into a CD or DVD casing. Customers forward photographs, and Rupert and Peter make the thumbnail card and return it.

1 Which THREE of the following are most likely to be external stakeholders in Klikfit?
   (a) Rupert and Peter, (b) suppliers of the card on which thumbnails are printed,
   (c) the government, which takes income tax from Rupert and Peter, (d) the bank
   where Klikfit has its account, (e) the owners of the business. *(3 marks)*

2 Choose the appropriate sector of industry — primary, secondary or tertiary — for each of the following organisations connected with this business.
   (a) Klikfit
   (b) suppliers of the card on which thumbnails are printed
   (c) manufacturers of the card on which thumbnails are printed
   (d) the business that fells the trees that make the card *(4 marks)*

3 One stakeholder group is the customers of the business.
   (a) Suggest TWO things that customers want from a business like Klikfit.
   (b) Explain how customers can influence a business like Klikfit. *(4 marks)*

4 A local children's charity has asked Klikfit for a special rate. A charity organisation is an example of social enterprise. Which TWO of the following are in the same category?
   (a) co-operatives, (b) multinationals, (c) mutual societies, (d) monopolies. *(2 marks)*

5 Explain what is meant by a 'gap in the market'. *(1 mark)*

6 Which of the following is the most likely effect on the market if this business succeeds?
   (a) It will shrink.
   (b) It will attract competitors.
   (c) The number of businesses in the market will get smaller.
   (d) It will become more profitable. *(1 mark)*

7 (a) State a suitable aim for Klikfit. *(1 mark)*
   (b) Explain why this is a relevant aim for Rupert and Peter's business. *(2 marks)*
   (c) Explain how Rupert and Peter could use objectives to help them reach their aim. *(2 marks)*

Total: 20 marks

Business ownership and location

Topic 6

Legal structures for small businesses

What the specification requires

You should know and understand that there are different types of business ownership and that small businesses tend to be limited to **sole trader**, **partnership** and **private limited company**. You need to understand what is meant by **limited liability** and how this can be of benefit to a business. You need to understand how, in each type, control, profit, management and other features will differ.

In brief

Only certain types of legal structure are appropriate for small businesses. The simplest structure is the one-person business called the sole trader. Partnerships are agreements between two or more people to share the responsibilities and organisation of the business — and also to share workload and profits (or losses). Both of these have the drawback of unlimited **liability** for the owners and a lack of continuity for the business. Private limited companies bring the owners the benefit of limiting their liability, but could also bring them problems by introducing more stakeholders, with different aims and objectives for the business.

Partnerships draw on the expertise and resources of more than one person

Revision notes

- A sole trader is a business that is owned and run by one person who raises the finance himself or herself, from personal sources (own funds) or by borrowing. The owner has sole control of the business, makes all the decisions and receives any profit. Sole traders gain from being independent. Raising more finance is often hard, so expanding the business may be difficult.
- A partnership is a business owned by two or more people jointly. Partnerships benefit from shared responsibility and extra expertise. Owners raise the finance themselves, from personal sources or by borrowing. The joint owners receive any profit and share risk equally unless a deed of partnership states otherwise.
- Sole traders and partnerships are easy to set up and can keep finances private.
- Owners are personally responsible for all the debts of the business. Each owner has unlimited liability and is responsible for debts up to the whole extent that he or she is able to pay. This means that their personal possessions may be at risk. If owners cannot pay, they may be made bankrupt. Liability means the responsibility of the owner for the debts of the business. It is possible to limit this.
- Private limited companies have limited liability. This can be of benefit to the business's reputation, but banks may be reluctant to lend to small companies, without guarantees. Private companies have to be legally established and registered at Companies House. They must produce certain accounts, which are available to the public. If the business cannot pay its debts, it may fail. For a company, this is called insolvency.
- A company has a legal existence separate from its owners, so it can be passed to different owners. This is called continuity.

In a nutshell

* Smaller businesses are likely to be organised as sole traders, partnerships or private limited companies.
* Each legal type is suitable for a small business.
* Sole traders carry all the responsibility themselves, but gain all of any profit.
* Partners share both responsibility and profit
* Private companies protect themselves by limiting liability.

Speak the language

sole trader — a business with unlimited liability, owned and run by one person

partnership — a business with unlimited liability, owned and run by two or more people

private limited company — a business with shareholders that has limited liability

limited liability — when liability is limited to the amount a shareholder invested

liability — the responsibility of the owner for the debts of the business

Boost your grade

AO1 to AO2: you should be able to compare the suitability of particular types of ownership for particular businesses. It is also important not only to understand limited liability, but also to decide whether or not it is appropriate for a business. A small business with little or no debt may not need to limit its liability.

Test yourself

Try this exam-style question.

Sarah is considering setting up a hairdressing business. She will need £25,000 to start it and intends to employ one full-time and two or three part-time staff. She has discussed either setting up on her own, or going into partnership with someone else.

1 What are the advantages of being a sole trader? *(3 marks)*

2 What are the advantages of partnership? *(3 marks)*

3 Would you recommend that Sarah sets up as a sole trader or partnership? Explain your answer. *(2 marks)*

Topic 7

Public limited companies

What the specification requires

You should understand that private limited companies may decide to become public limited companies for a number of reasons. There are benefits and drawbacks to such a move, which you should be able to explain. You will not be asked about the legal process of incorporation.

In brief

Private limited companies already benefit from limited liability, so the main reason for them to become public is likely to be to raise extra finance. It is also possible, however, for the original owners to lose control to new shareholders. For some private limited companies, this change in organisation will be an appropriate route to take; for others, drawbacks will outweigh gains.

Revision notes

- **A private limited company** that wants to raise large amounts of capital may do so by becoming a public limited company.
- Private limited companies are usually shortened to 'ltd'; **public limited companies** are usually shortened to 'plc'.
- Becoming a plc is neither expensive nor complicated; it involves producing evidence that the business is in good health and reliable.
- Becoming a plc allows the business to offer shares for sale on the stock exchange. It is a good way to raise large amounts of finance. However, a stock exchange listing means anyone can buy shares — including people or organisations that may put their own interests

above those of the business. Competitors who buy shares have information about the business, but also have a say in how it is organised or operated. Public shareholders are often more interested in gaining a quick profit than in the long-term health of the business, so they may buy and sell shares regardless of the strength of the business. This can be a drawback for the plc.

- Plcs also have to publish annual accounts and make them accessible to anyone who requests them. This means that all their strengths and weaknesses can easily be seen, even by competitors.
- **Shareholders** each have a vote (one per share), so they can affect the decision-making process of the business at the annual general meeting of the company.

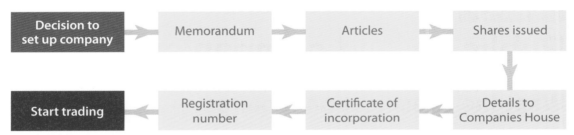

Setting up a company (note: there are plans by the government to make this process even easier)

In a nutshell

* Private limited companies may need extra finance to grow.
* One way to raise this is by going public.
* There are advantages to this, such as raising finance.
* There are also disadvantages, such as the possibility of losing control.

Boost your grade   **AO1 to AO2:** for AO2 marks you must show that you understand concepts in context. You should only suggest becoming a plc as a way to raise money for a large business that is already succeeding. It is not suitable for start-up or small businesses.

Test yourself

Fill in the missing words using the list below. If you are feeling confident, cover the words and do the exercise from memory.

Becoming a .... allows the business to offer .... for sale on the

.... It is a good way to raise large amounts of finance. However, there are some disadvantages. Public companies have to publish .... and make them accessible to anyone who requests them. .... who buy shares have .... about the business and a say in how it is ...., ... may be more interested in gaining a quick .... than in the .... health of the business.

annual accounts   competitors   information   long-term
organised   plc   profit   shareholders   shares   stock exchange

Topic 8

Integration and growth

What the specification requires

You will need to know how businesses grow through integration and be able to describe horizontal, vertical, lateral and conglomerate integration. You should understand the advantages that a business might gain from integration. You should be able to explain the difference between a merger and a takeover.

In brief

Integration is one of the ways in which a business may grow. It means one business joining with another by either merger or takeover. The type of integration depends on the relative position of the two businesses in the chain of production, and in their own markets. Mergers are where the two companies are equal partners and agree to join together. Takeovers are where one company buys out another.

Revision notes

- A business can get bigger through either **internal growth** or **external growth**. Internal or organic growth is when the business grows larger from within by increasing sales, using new technology, widening its product range or expanding its markets.
- External growth is when a business grows by joining with other businesses. It can join with other businesses in an agreed marriage or **merger**, or in a hostile way in a forced marriage or **takeover**. When a business joins with another, this is termed **integration**.

HSBC is an example of a company that has expanded through external growth

- A business may join with another business:
  - at the same stage of production (e.g. one bakery with another) — this is horizontal integration
  - at a previous stage of production (e.g. a bakery with a flour mill or wheat grower) — this is backward vertical integration
  - at a later stage of production (e.g. a bakery with a bread shop) — this is forward vertical integration
  - in a similar but not directly related market but one that has some link with the product (e.g. a bakery with a sandwich shop) — this is lateral integration
  - in an unrelated area (e.g. a bakery with a bicycle manufacturer) — this is conglomerate integration or diversification
- Integration may bring advantages to the larger business. It could mean a bigger market share, access to new markets, economies of scale, better terms from suppliers and benefits from sharing technology. If a business enters new markets — or diversifies — this takes it into new markets and new challenges. It may even be that it needs to do this because its core business is in decline.
- Integration could also mean the removal of competitors and therefore the ability to charge higher prices. This could be a disadvantage for consumers.
- Businesses can also grow by franchising. This means selling the right to use a successful product or business model. Franchisees buy the **franchise** from the franchiser. They pay a fee plus a royalty, which is a percentage of their turnover.

Speak the language

internal growth — (also called organic growth) when a business grows larger from within

external growth — when a business grows by joining with other businesses

merger — two businesses agreeing to join together

takeover — one business buying out another

integration — the technical term used when two businesses join together

franchise — expansion through selling the right to use a successful business model

In a nutshell

* Businesses can grow internally or externally.
* Internal growth is called organic growth.
* External growth involves joining with other businesses, or integration.
* If it is an agreed marriage, this is a merger.
* If it is opposed, it is a takeover.
* Integration can happen in different directions, up, down or across the chain of production.

Boost your grade

AO2 to AO3: sometimes you will be asked to make recommendations. Would it be wise, for example, for the business you have been given to merge with another and, if so, in what direction? Remember, there is not always a right answer. AO3 marks are more for supporting a decision and recommendation than for actually making it.

Test yourself

Using the bakery example, complete the diagram to show the different types of integration.

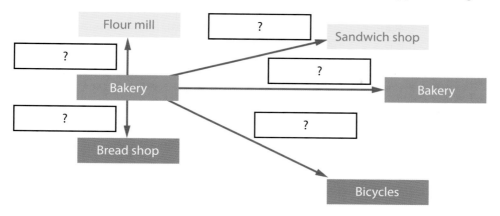

Multinationals

What the specification requires

This topic concentrates on multinational companies, but you will also need to know about charities and not-for-profit organisations as possible ways to own and run a business. These are covered in Topic 4. You should understand that there are both advantages and disadvantages to multinationals (and their stakeholders), and should be able to explain these.

In brief

A multinational is a business that has operations in many countries around the world. Often a multinational is the result of conglomerate growth (see Topic 8). Usually, this can also be taken to mean production facilities on a global scale. It also tends to mean a global brand. Many multinationals are holding companies. These are companies that hold shares in other companies in the same group. A typical multinational could look like the one shown in the diagram overleaf.

Revision notes

- The multinational shown is organised as a **holding company**. Atlantic Holdings (the holding company or **parent company**) holds all or most of the shares in each of the **operating companies** (e.g. Windpower plc). Operating companies are known as **subsidiaries**. Often they will have their own directors and their shares may be traded on local stock exchanges: for example, shares in US subsidiary Topp Hotels Inc. might be traded on the New York Stock Exchange.

- Multinationals can gain from being big. They can buy in bulk (i.e. very large amounts). They can also locate operations to keep costs and taxation down. Sometimes production has to be based in certain areas to access markets that would otherwise be barred to them — this has brought several businesses into the European Union. Some businesses are almost bound to be multinationals — oil, for example, has to be discovered, extracted, refined and then sold worldwide.

- A multinational may decide to pay tax in the country where its headquarters is based — which could be a country that has low business taxation — rather than where it actually operates. It can also take advantage of local low labour costs and less strict labour laws. Multinationals have come into conflict with human rights groups, who see them as exploiting labour or natural resources in poorer countries in order to boost profits in richer ones. Companies have been accused of destroying the environment and exploiting labour for profit, as well as supporting certain governments and opposing others for their own advantage.

- Multinationals also benefit from global brands. A global brand is a brand image that is recognised throughout the world. This helps multinationals to compete against local businesses. Brands are of immense value to a business; they help it to be recognised and to gain new markets.

Structure of a typical multinational

In a nutshell

- ✳ Holding companies are a way for a business to keep control over a number of other businesses.
- ✳ Multinationals are often organised in this way.
- ✳ Multinationals operate in a number of countries.
- ✳ Sometimes they are more rich and powerful than the countries where they operate, and this can cause problems.
- ✳ They are often criticised for avoiding tax, taking advantage of cheap labour and destroying the environment.
- ✳ Multinationals would defend themselves against these charges.

Speak the language

holding company — a company that holds all or most of the shares in other companies

parent company — another name for the top company in a group

operating company — a company that produces and trades

subsidiary — a business that is owned by a holding company

Test yourself

In the BrandZ Top 100 ratings, Google jumped to become the top brand by value in 2008 and stayed in this position in 2009. Use Google to see if you can find out which are currently the top brands and how many of them are multinationals.

Rank 2009	Rank 2008	Brand	BV 2009 ($m)	BV 2008 ($m)
1	=	Google	100,039	86,057
2	+1	Microsoft	76,249	70,887
3	+1	Coca-Cola	67,625	58,208
4	+2	IBM	66,622	55,335
5	+3	McDonald's	66,575	49,499
6	+1	Apple	63,113	55,206
7	−2	China Mobile	61,283	57,225
8	−6	GE (General Electric)	59,793	71,379
9	+2	Vodafone	53,727	36,962
10	=	Marlboro	49,460	37,324

Source: www.branz.com. Note: the 'Rank 2008' column shows movement from 2008 to 2009. BV = brand value

Topic 10

Location

What the specification requires

You will need to understand what influences the location of business at local, national and international levels. You may be asked to review location factors that you are given, and to make a decision or recommendation about location.

In brief

The location of a business is a vital factor in its ability to be successful. A business dealing directly with customers, for example, would soon find itself in trouble if customers could not access it because of its location. Different location factors are going to be of greater or lesser importance to a business, depending on the nature of the business and its markets. Businesses may be providing goods or services directly to consumers, or may be involved in manufacturing, processing or production. Location factors include the cost, amount and suitability of available land and labour, and the availability of government or other external assistance.

Revision notes

- Some businesses use natural resources, so they need to be near them. The size and quality of the site and the availability of **infrastructure** (power, transport links, etc.) may be as important as its location. The size, quality and structure of the labour force are also important. Government help may come in the form of grants, subsidies or lower rates.
- External bodies such as the European Union may provide benefits that encourage businesses to locate in certain areas. Internationally, such benefits may also include lower taxation, or laws that make it easier for the business to work in a particular country.
- For a business supplying directly to consumers, location factors include accessibility, local services, rates, rents and the presence of competition. Certain services, such as a local shop, bank or hairdresser's, will be located as near to customers as possible. In other cases, the service will be located at a particular place due to geographical factors (e.g. holiday destinations) or due to the specialist nature of the service (you would not expect a heart surgeon to come to you).
- Manufacturing locations are influenced by factors such as how near production needs to be to raw materials, or to consumers. There will be a certain amount of 'pull' in both directions. A **bulk-decreasing** industry will need to be as near to raw material sources as possible. Oil refining is an example.
- The manufacture of pottery, however, is a **bulk-increasing** industry — china clay is easily transported but finished goods need to be carefully packaged and are expensive to transport, as they have grown in bulk. Such a business therefore needs to be located near its market.

Speak the language

infrastructure — the 'web' of services that support an economy (e.g. power, transport, communications)

bulk-decreasing — means that the good becomes easier to transport once processed

bulk-increasing — means that the good gets bigger or bulkier once processed and becomes harder to transport

In a nutshell

* Some businesses have little choice about location, as they need to be near raw materials or resources. Sea fishing, for example, must take place at sea!
* Other businesses may need to be near their market (e.g. services).
* To keep costs down, it is better to locate where the most expensive form of transport is used only for the shortest distance.
* Bulk-increasing industries locate near to markets; bulk-decreasing ones locate near to resources.

Boost your grade

AO1 to AO2: you should be able to consider the various factors that are either pulling or pushing a business towards a particular location. There will be the pull of the market, for example. To achieve AO2, you must make sure that these are appropriate to the business example you are using.

Test yourself

Fill in the missing words using the list below. If you are feeling confident, cover the words and do the exercise from memory.

The production process takes goods from .... to .... Sometimes this involves a decrease in volume, sometimes an increase. A .... industry is one where the product becomes harder to transport as it passes through the process. An example is .... being turned into .... A .... industry is one where the product becomes easier to transport as it passes through the process. An example is .... being turned into .... The business should locate where .... will be ....

bulk-decreasing   **transport costs**   **apple juice**   **lowest**   **furniture**

bulk-increasing   **apples**   **finished product**   **wood**   **raw materials**

Topic 11
Public corporations

What the specification requires

Public corporations are just one of the ways of owning a business that you need to know about. You should understand why they have a place as a type of business structure in the UK economy.

In brief

'The public sector' refers to those businesses and enterprises that are owned not by the public, but by local or national government on behalf of the public. Many of these are services that could not be funded by the private sector or where it is difficult to make economic charges. Sometimes, other considerations such as national security (the police and armed forces) or accessibility for all (the National Health Service) are important.

Previously a nationalised company, BT was privatised in 1984

Revision notes

- Public corporations are businesses that are owned by the government, which provides finance and determines policy. They are run, however, by independent boards (although members of these may be appointed by the government).
- Some corporations arise where an industry has been **nationalised** — that is, taken from private ownership into the public sector — while others will never have been in the private sector, having been established and funded by government from the start. This latter group includes organisations such as the BBC (set up with a charter). While, at one time, most of the major industries in the country had been nationalised (including coal, shipbuilding, iron and steel, water, gas and telecommunications), the trend towards the end of the twentieth century was to return these to the private sector through the process of **privatisation**.
- In some cases, it is difficult to make **economic charges** for a service. For example, street lighting benefits everyone within a particular area, but it is not possible to charge each individual for his or her use of the service. The service is therefore provided by local authorities and paid for through council tax. Other local authority services include libraries, parks and gardens, museums and some control over schools (although budgets are now being more and more given to individual schools rather than to the local authority).
- Public goods are those for which it would not be possible to make an economic charge, such as street lighting and roads; merit goods are those which governments feel that they ought to provide for social reasons, otherwise people will not make enough use of them. These include education and the health service.

In a nutshell

* Some businesses are owned by the government.
* Owned on behalf of the public, so are called 'the public sector'.
* Some of these businesses are the result of nationalisation.
* Some were set up by government originally.
* Some have been sold back into the private sector.
* Reasons for public sector businesses are often social.

Speak the language

nationalisation — the process of taking business into public ownership

privatisation — the process of selling business to the private sector

economic charges — charges for fair use of a product

Test yourself

Match the word or phrase on the left with the most appropriate word or phrase on the right.

1	BBC	owned by government
2	economic charges	taken into public ownership
3	local authority services	sold into private ownership
4	merit goods	charges for fair use
5	nationalisation	council tax
6	privatisation	social reasons
7	public corporation	can't charge for them
8	public goods	charter

Boost your grade

AO2 to AO3: talking about the Private Finance Initiative (PFI) as a way of using private money and government money side by side — and its effect on areas like the National Health Service — will earn you AO3 marks.

Section test: Business ownership and location

Read the passage and answer the questions.

Redfix plc quarries stone from a number of quarries in the east of England. It supplies crushed stone to be used for road and footpath bases. Its main customer is therefore public sector businesses. It also produces a small quantity of high-quality stone that can be polished and made into jewellery. Sarah has just finished a jewellery course at college and is considering setting up a small jewellery business.

1   Redfix is a plc. Complete the following passage using the words provided.

Becoming a plc allowed the business to offer .... for sale on the .... It enabled Redfix to raise large amounts of .... However, there are some disadvantages. Public companies like Redfix have to publish .... and make them accessible to anyone who requests them. .... who buy shares have information about the business and a say in how it is run.

   shares   finance   competitors   stock exchange   annual accounts

(5 marks)

2   Outline the main factor that has influenced Redfix's location.   *(1 mark)*

3   Define 'the public sector'.   *(1 mark)*

4   Bluegrade, a competitor which quarries stone in the south of England, wants to merge with Redfix.
   (a) Explain what type of integration this represents.   *(2 marks)*
   (b) Explain one benefit that the combined business could gain.   *(2 marks)*

5   Sarah is considering setting up a jewellery business. She has discussed either setting up on her own, or going into partnership with someone else.
   (a) What are the advantages of being a sole trader?   *(3 marks)*
   (b) What are the advantages of partnership?   *(3 marks)*
   (c) Would you recommend that Sarah sets up as a sole trader or a partnership? Give reasons for your judgement.   *(3 marks)*

Total: 20 marks

Check your answers online at:
www.hodderplus.co.uk/philipallan

Topic 12

Recruitment and selection

What the specification requires

You need to know how a business recruits and selects, including the use of job descriptions, person specifications and the interview process. You should understand that there are many sources of information that can help in selection, and that each business will use those appropriate to its own situation.

In brief

Recruitment and selection describes the process by which a business finds new staff. The human resources area of the business usually handles this. This may be a separate department (perhaps called 'personnel') or may be just one of the jobs done by a manager or owner. In most cases, the process is the same. A need is identified, a job is advertised and a selection process is followed by an appointment.

Revision notes

- **Recruitment** is the process by which a business finds new employees. The business may need full- or part-time employees. Even small businesses may need to recruit employees. Sometimes staff are taken on because they have been recommended. Usually appointment follows a process.
- Recruitment needs to take place when a need for new staff is identified by the business. There are a number of reasons why a business might need new staff:

Retirement creates a need for recruitment

- The business could be getting bigger.
- Staff could have left.
- The business may need new skills.

■ The business has to decide whether to recruit from outside the business (**external recruitment**) or to train its own staff (**internal recruitment**). If it decides to recruit, the process is as follows:
  - It identifies the job that needs doing and writes a **job description** to show what tasks, skills and qualifications are needed.
  - It writes a **person specification** to show the type of person it needs to recruit.
  - The selection process usually starts with an advertisement. This must be placed in the right place to attract the right applicants. Applicants may be asked for **CVs**, letters of support and references. **Short-listed** applicants are invited to interview. Interviews in a small business are likely to be one-to-one; in larger businesses they could be in front of a panel. They could also involve tests, group or team activities, and/or presentations. After the interviews the best candidate is offered the job.

■ Recruiting can be very expensive. Sometimes no candidate is good enough for the job and the whole process has to be repeated. This is why businesses try to make sure they get it right first time.

Speak the language

recruitment — the process of selecting and employing staff

external recruitment — recruiting from outside the business

internal recruitment — recruiting from inside the business

job description — shows what tasks, skills and qualifications are needed

person specification — shows the type of person the business needs to recruit

CV — curriculum vitae; an applicant's record of skills, experience and qualifications

short list — the applicants most likely to be good at the job; these will be interviewed

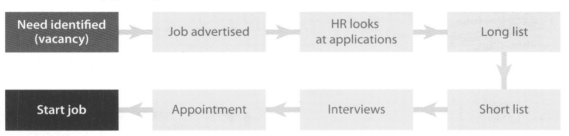

| Need identified (vacancy) | → | Job advertised | → | HR looks at applications | → | Long list |
| Start job | ← | Appointment | ← | Interviews | ← | Short list |

The recruitment process

In a nutshell

* Even the smallest businesses may need employees.
* The recruitment process may be informal (e.g. by recommendation).
* Recruitment may be a formal process from job advertisement through interview to appointment.
* Some posts may be filled through internal recruitment, some by external recruitment. Each method has benefits and drawbacks.

Test yourself

Fill in the missing words using the list below. If you are feeling confident, cover the words and do the exercise from memory.

The business will write a .... to show what tasks, skills and qualifications are needed and a .... to show the sort of worker that will fit the requirements. It .... the post and invites .... Using .... and .... that are sent in, it draws up a .... of the .... it thinks are best qualified. These become .... and are invited to .... The successful .... is offered the job.

advertises   applicants   applications   candidates   CVs   interview   interviewee   letters of application   job description   person specification   short list

Topic 13

Training and appraisal

What the specification requires

You should understand that there are different reasons why workers need training and different types of training appropriate to the employee's position in the business. You should also know that staff appraisal is central to good motivation and to staff development.

In brief

Training is the process of making sure that workers in a business have the knowledge and skills necessary to do the job. It is seen as a benefit to the business. It is necessary to make sure that the business is operating as efficiently as possible. **Development** is different from training. It is seen as being of more benefit to the worker — developing his or her own skills and knowledge. Development may involve, for example, taking professional examinations or undertaking further study.

Speak the language

training — developing the skills and knowledge needed by the business

development — developing skills and knowledge to improve the worker

induction training — initial or introductory training

appraisal — the process used to see how well a worker is doing

Revision notes

- All new appointments to a business require some form of **induction training**. This is training to introduce staff to the workplace and the job. It includes basic training in processes and methods, and also lets the new employee know what is 'usual' in the business. This is called 'custom and practice' and covers issues such as when breaks or leave can be taken, and the basic operation of the workplace.

- Businesses have to decide whether to carry out training themselves, or use external agencies. Agencies can be more effective at training, but tend to be expensive. Big businesses will have their own training departments. Further training may therefore be either:
  - On-the-job training at the place of work. This often involves being shown what to do by an experienced employee. This is cheaper than using external trainers, but may result in mistakes and waste.
  - Off-the-job training, off site. This is usually with professional trainers. It is more expensive in both time and money, but may provide better training.

- **Appraisal** is the process used to see how well a worker is doing. It also allows the worker to exchange views with his or her employer. A good appraisal may result in rewards, or may be part of the path to promotion. Most businesses that have invested a lot in time and training and development in staff will want to keep them and may operate a system of financial or other rewards (such as recognition and increased responsibility) in order to do so. Appraisal can help to identify where progress has been made.

- Many businesses nowadays expect employees to keep retraining and improving skills. This is called lifelong learning.

Training and development

In a nutshell

* Training is the process of making sure that workers can do the job.
* Training is of benefit to the business.
* Development is of more benefit to the worker — developing his or her own skills and knowledge.
* Induction training is necessary when a worker starts at a business.
* Appraisal allows employer and employee to exchange views, and recognises training and development needs.
* Many workers need to train continuously as businesses change.
* This is called lifelong learning.

Test yourself

Choose the most appropriate answer from each of the following alternatives.

1 The process to develop the skills and knowledge that the business needs is called **(a)** recruitment, **(b)** training, **(c)** advertising, **(d)** interviewing, **(e)** development.

2 The process to develop the skills and knowledge that the employee needs is called **(a)** recruitment, **(b)** training, **(c)** advertising, **(d)** interviewing, **(e)** development.

3 An employee's initial introduction to a business is usually called **(a)** initial training, **(b)** introduction training, **(c)** induction training, **(d)** initial development, **(e)** introductory development.

4 The process to see how well a worker is doing and suggest improvements is called **(a)** praise, **(b)** interviewing, **(c)** induction, **(d)** personal development, **(e)** appraisal.

5 Training that takes place throughout the worker's employment is called **(a)** lifelong learning, **(b)** lifelong education, **(c)** large as life learning, **(d)** large as life education, **(e)** college training.

AO2 to AO3: can you recognise the conflict of interest between training and development? A business may be keen to train a worker in its own methods and operations. This makes the worker more valuable to the business. On the other hand, the business may be reluctant to encourage development, as this makes the worker more flexible and more attractive to other businesses. Making a case for either takes you into AO3 marks.

Topic 14
Payment methods

What the specification requires

You will need to understand that pay can be used to motivate staff. You should realise, however, that most employees will only work for a certain basic rate of pay, and it is only payments made in addition to this that might be motivators. You may be asked to work out payments from figures you are given.

In brief

It is vital to workers to know, firstly, that they will be paid for work done, and secondly, how they will be

Fotolia

The most common 'perk' is a company car

paid. This allows them to plan their expenditure and lifestyle with certainty. Different methods of payment reward different types of work and efficiency, and are therefore used by different businesses according to their circumstances. To ensure flexibility, a business might use part-time staff rather than full-time employees. It will also make the choice between employing the specialists it needs all the time, and bringing outside expertise in when required.

Revision notes

- **Remuneration** refers to the way a worker is paid. Each type of payment system impacts on the business by motivating workers to be more efficient. There are also problems with each system, as suggested below.
- Piece rates reward manufacturing workers for the number of items made. This can encourage speed but may be at the expense of quality or accuracy.
- Time rates are paid at an amount per period of time worked. The most common are weekly or monthly wages, or annual salaries. Workers who are paid a wage can normally earn **overtime** for extra time completed. Those on a salary have their annual amount divided by 12 months and receive this regardless of hours worked. Time rates can lead to workers working more slowly, but perhaps more accurately.
- Commission is a reward paid for increased sales. It is usually set as a percentage of all sales made above a base amount. This encourages salespeople to sell, but may lead to customer dissatisfaction if too much pressure is used. It can also lead to low (sometimes no) wages for those salespeople who do not exceed the base target.
- Businesses need to employ a mixture of staff so that they have flexibility. They may employ full-time staff for positions where this is necessary and part-time staff to cover busy periods. They may also employ freelancers or other outside specialists to bring special skills to the business when needed.
- Other benefits may also form part of a remuneration package. These are often called 'perks' or 'fringe benefits', as they do not form a central part of the pay package. These could include items such as pensions, company cars, canteens, staff discounts, **profit sharing** and annual bonus payments.

> ### Speak the language
>
> **remuneration** — the package of pay and benefits that is the reward for working for a business
>
> **overtime** — extra pay for extra time worked, usually paid at a higher rate than normal time (time and a half, or double time)
>
> **profit sharing** — when some profit is shared among workers as a reward for their efforts

In a nutshell

- Remuneration refers to the way in which workers are paid.
- Most payments are in money; some are through 'perks'.
- Different systems are appropriate to different businesses.
- Each system has benefits and drawbacks.
- Businesses choose systems to give them efficiency and flexibility.

AO2 to AO3: for AO3 marks you should be able to discuss the decisions that businesses have to make to keep wage costs down but remain flexible and efficient. For example, when would it be better to employ a freelance expert rather than have an expert employee on the books? You should also be able to consider the pros and cons of types of payments — does commission lead to pressure selling? Do piece rates lead to poor quality?

Test yourself

Match the term on the left to its correct description on the right.

1	commission	the way in which a worker is paid
2	freelancer	an amount paid per period of time worked
3	perks	an amount paid for the number of items made
4	piece rate	an amount paid for increased sales
5	remuneration	a person who offers his or her services to businesses on a temporary basis
6	time rate	benefits such as company cars, pension schemes and staff discounts

Topic 15

Motivation and the working environment

What the specification requires

You need to know both why and how a business might try to motivate its employees. This topic looks at how a business can motivate through methods other than money, including the creation of an appropriate working environment. You will not be asked specific questions about theories, but can use your knowledge of them to support your answers.

In brief

Businesses are keen to motivate workers — that is, to persuade them to work harder or more efficiently. If the workers are more efficient, so is the business, so it is likely to be more profitable. Businesses can try to keep labour motivated by keeping employees happy. This could be done by rewards (other than money), by making the job more interesting, or just by creating an environment in which people want to work. This can include using appropriate management styles.

Revision notes

- Businesses can motivate workers by changing the nature of their job. Ideas include:
  - **Job rotation** — encouraging workers to do a number of different jobs and move from one job to another at regular intervals. This helps to maintain their interest in the work.
  - **Job enrichment** — giving the employee greater responsibility. For example, a production worker will work better as part of a team making a product than if he or she sees just a small part of the process. The worker can see the whole job and its importance, and so will be motivated. Team working in this way is linked to 'cell production', where each team or 'cell' produces an entire product.
  - **Job enlargement** — increasing the employee's range of responsibilities and/or skills.
- Managers can operate different **leadership styles** to make a better working environment. If they are good managers, they will vary the style according to the situation. The main styles are:
  - Autocratic: managers instruct and direct. This may demotivate workers.
  - Laissez-faire: managers allow employees to express views and argue a case. This can be more motivating, but may lead to a lack of central direction or purpose — managers may even be pulling in different directions.
  - Democratic: managers allow staff to participate in decision making, leading to more motivation and job satisfaction; however, this may also be inefficient.
  - Bureaucratic: managers make decisions according to a rigid set of rules. This can destroy interest, innovation and motivation.
  - Paternalistic: managers take the welfare of workers into account when making decisions. The main drawback is that managers' and workers' ideas of what is best for the employees may not coincide.
- In the real world, a great deal of motivation can be and is provided through praise and recognition of a job well done.

Ingram

In a nutshell

- ∗ Businesses are keen to motivate workers to work harder.
- ∗ This can be achieved partly through providing good working conditions.
- ∗ Businesses can also change the jobs that workers do to keep them interested.
- ∗ Managers can use different styles to motivate workers.
- ∗ The style chosen needs to be suitable to be effective.

Speak the language

job rotation — letting workers do a number of different jobs to maintain interest in the work

job enrichment — giving the employee greater responsibility, where each team or 'cell' produces an entire product

job enlargement — increasing the employee's range of responsibilities and/or skills

leadership styles — the way managers operate

Test yourself

Match the management styles on the left with the descriptions on the right.

1	paternalistic	instruct and direct
2	laissez-faire	allow staff to participate in decision making
3	democratic	make decisions according to a rigid set of rules
4	bureaucratic	allow employees to express views
5	autocratic	consider the welfare of workers when making decisions

Fotolia

Health and safety signs have to be clear

Topic 16
Businesses and legislation

What the specification requires

You need to understand that there are various laws to protect workers and that employers have certain responsibilities to their employees. You should be aware of key legislation in the area of employment rights, including health and safety, discrimination, equal pay and minimum wages. You will not be asked to quote or remember titles and dates of specific Acts.

In brief

Employees in a business have certain rights in law. They also have responsibilities. Employers also have rights and responsibilities regarding their employees. Workers have a right to decent and safe working conditions and fair pay for the work they undertake. Employers have the right to expect employees to be punctual, efficient and loyal, and the responsibility to provide good working conditions and fair pay. Many rights are laid down in law.

Revision notes

- Basic **employment rights** include the right to:
  - safe, healthy and reasonably comfortable working conditions
  - protection from danger in the workplace
  - breaks and holidays
- Most of these rights are laid down in employment law. Employees, by law, are entitled to:
  - a written statement giving rates of pay, terms and conditions of employment, pensions, notice periods and disciplinary procedures
  - join a trade union
  - the **minimum wage**
  - a detailed pay statement
  - **redundancy** payments
  - take part in the management of the business for which they work (under EU law)
  - not be unfairly dismissed
- The main law regarding health and safety is the 1974 Health and Safety at Work Act (HASAW). There must be proper washroom and toilet facilities, ventilation, fire exits and good levels of heating and lighting for all workers. Employers must fit guards to dangerous machines.
- The law states that in all matters of recruitment, selection, training, promotion and other areas of human resources there should be no **discrimination**. This includes the right to equal pay for equal work or responsibility. The main laws cover:
  - Equal pay (1970). Men and women should receive equal pay for equal work.
  - Sex discrimination (1975). This extended equality to include recruitment, training and promotion opportunities.
  - Race relations (1976). This made discrimination on the grounds of race or colour, nationality or ethnic group illegal. It set up the Commission for Racial Equality (now part of the Equality and Human Rights Commission) to investigate complaints.
  - Disability discrimination (1995). Employers of 20 people or more cannot discriminate on grounds of disability.
  - Age discrimination (2006). Employers cannot exclude people from jobs because of their age.
- There are arrangements to deal with employers and employees when employment law is, or may have been, broken. Employment tribunals sit to decide if either side has broken the law and may then award compensation or levy fines.

In a nutshell

* Workers are entitled to basic rights from employers.
* Employers also have rights, along with their responsibilities.
* Workers should work in safe, healthy environments.
* They should be paid at least the minimum wage.
* There should be no discrimination in employment.
* Employment tribunals rule on whether or not the law has been broken.

Speak the language

employment rights — the rights of workers

minimum wage — the least that, by law, an employer can pay

redundancy — when a person's job is no longer needed

discrimination — acting against someone for a reason they cannot control

Test yourself

Choose the most appropriate answer from each of following alternatives.

1 One basic employment right is the right to working conditions that **(a)** are safe, **(b)** are convenient, **(c)** have parking, **(d)** are colourful.

2 Workers also have the right to leisure through breaks and **(a)** television, **(b)** holidays, **(c)** gym membership, **(d)** cinema.

3 The main law regarding health and safety is **(a)** the 1954 Health and Safety at Work Act, **(b)** the 1974 Health and Comfort at Work Act, **(c)** the 1974 Health and Safety at Work Act, **(d)** the 1924 Healthy Workers Act.

4 The law states that there should be no discrimination on grounds of all of the following EXCEPT **(a)** gender, **(b)** race, **(c)** height, **(d)** age.

5 Employees are entitled to be paid at least **(a)** the going rate, **(b)** the maximum wage, **(c)** the bonus wage, **(d)** the minimum wage.

Boost your grade

AO1: you will not be asked to name specific employment legislation, but it will show good knowledge, for AO1 marks, if you can accurately name the Health and Safety at Work Act 1974 and some of its features, or a specific anti-discrimination law.

Topic 17
Industrial relations

What the specification requires

You need to understand that trade unions represent workers, fight for better conditions and also act as pressure groups. You should be aware of the different types of industrial disputes and how they may be resolved, including the role of ACAS and the reasons for single union agreements.

In brief

Industrial relations refers to the relationship between the employer and the employer's representatives, and the employee and the employee's representatives. Employer groups may be professional associations, employer associations or bodies representing particular industries. Employee groups are usually trade unions. Trade unions also act as pressure groups, seeking changes in the law to improve pay and working conditions, and act to protect the interests of their members.

Workers are allowed to join trade unions to fight for their rights

Revision notes

- Employee groups and employer groups often negotiate (try to come to an agreement) on pay and conditions of work. Because negotiations are taking place between representatives of groups, this is called **collective bargaining**.
- An **industrial dispute** is where there is a breakdown in industrial relations. An industrial dispute can lead to some kind of **industrial action** being taken by one side or the other.
- Employees can take various levels of industrial action. These include:
  - overtime bans
  - working to rule (production slowed as a result of all rules and regulations being followed to the letter)
  - go-slows (continuing with the job but at a much reduced rate)
- The most serious action is for employees to withdraw their labour altogether in a **strike**. Strikes may be selective, short (1-day strikes) or total. Striking workers may also **picket** to try to persuade others not to work. Strikes are damaging to both employers and employees.
- On the employer's side, those in dispute may, in certain cases, be dismissed or the employer may refuse to allow them to work (a 'lock-out').
- Because such tactics are so damaging, there are laws to try to stop industrial disputes getting worse. Should negotiations break down, there are bodies in place to help. The main body is the Advisory, Conciliation and Arbitration Service (ACAS), which provides a service to help solve industrial disputes through negotiation and agreement. It can:
  - advise
  - conciliate — try to get the two sides to agree
  - arbitrate — make a ruling between the two sides
- In some businesses a single union agreement is negotiated so that the employers have to deal with just one union. This benefits employers, but it may also may help workers, if everyone is represented by the same union.

In a nutshell

* Collective bargaining is where employee groups and employer groups negotiate on pay and conditions of work.
* Industrial relations describes the relationship between employer and employee groups.
* Sometimes there is an industrial dispute when there is a breakdown in industrial relations.
* An industrial dispute can lead to industrial action such as overtime bans and strikes by employees or lock-outs by employers.
* The Advisory, Conciliation and Arbitration Service (ACAS) was set up to help solve industrial disputes.

Speak the language

industrial relations — the relationship between employers and employees

collective bargaining — when one representative group negotiates with another

industrial dispute — when these relations break down

industrial action — when one or other side uses tactics to try to force agreement

strike — withdrawal of labour

picket — a group of workers stationed at the entrance to a workplace to try and persuade others to support industrial action

Boost your grade

AO1 to AO2: not all industrial disputes lead to strike action, so do not assume that this is the only option. Most disputes are settled long before they reach this stage; to achieve AO2 marks, you should be able to discuss why this might be the case.

Test yourself

Try this exam-style question.

Jonathan Cross runs a textile business, weaving and dyeing fabric with large machines in a noisy factory. Recently, a number of workers have complained about the noise. They say they are thinking of joining a union, but Jonathan is discouraging them.

Explain two possible advantages that a trade union could bring to the workers at this business.

Section test: The workforce in business

Honecker Enterprises runs training courses for people who want to be youth group leaders. It is a small business, with two training managers and six other employees.

Recently, one manager has left, so Honecker Enterprises has recruited another.

1   Complete the sentences below by choosing the correct words from the list provided.
    (a) Applicants are asked to include their job histories, or ....
    (b) Honecker Enterprises looks at applications and draws up a .... for interview.
    (c) Those invited for interview become .... for the job.

candidates   short list   CVs

(3 marks)

2   Describe and outline the purpose of the following documents used in the recruitment process:
    (a) job description
    (b) person specification   *(6 marks)*

3   Which THREE of the following basic rights in law are enjoyed by all employees at Honecker Enterprises? **(a)** Free training in youth leadership whenever they want it, **(b)** protection from danger in the workplace, **(c)** safe, healthy and reasonably comfortable working conditions, **(d)** extra money to be paid for a job well done, **(e)** breaks and holidays.
    (3 marks)

4   Which THREE of the following are types of training? **(a)** Induction, **(b)** on the job, **(c)** interviewing, **(d)** lifelong learning, **(e)** personal development.   *(3 marks)*

5   Honecker's trainers earn a basic salary. They are encouraged to earn more through commission on sales of DVDs of training sessions.
    (a) Describe and explain 'commission' as a means of payment.   *(2 marks)*
    (b) Suggest and explain one advantage and one disadvantage of commission.   *(4 marks)*

6   Honecker's staff have complained that many of the jobs they do are boring and repetitive.
    (a) Suggest TWO ways in which Honecker could motivate staff by changing the nature of their jobs.   *(2 marks)*
    (b) Recommend which way Honecker should choose and explain why you think so.   *(2 marks)*

Total: 25 marks

Business organisation

Internal organisational structures

What the specification requires

You will need to understand how a business may be organised and that there are both formal and informal organisation structures within a business. You will need to show that you understand organisation charts and the positions, responsibilities and authority of those in them.

In brief

For any business or organisation to operate at all, it needs to have some sort of structure. Businesses are therefore organised in a number of different ways. How they are organised usually depends on their size, on the management style of the owners, or on the type of business or type of market that they operate in. Decision making could happen at the centre, or be delegated to managers throughout the organisation.

Revision notes

- **Organisational charts** can show how a business is organised. The most common type is the family tree chart, showing each 'family' of workers under a manager or director.
- Each manager has a number of people under his or her control. This is called the **span of control** and may be wide or narrow. The narrower the span, the stronger the power the manager has over those underneath — his or her **subordinates**. This power is usually called **authority** — that is, the right within the organisational set-up to make decisions. In some cases, this authority may be passed on; this is called **delegation.**
- Some organisations are controlled from the centre. This means that decisions are made by a few people. In an organisation that is very centrally controlled, there will be little delegation. This can mean quick decision making. But sometimes the centre is too far away from the customer to be efficient. Decentralised organisations spread decision making. This can mean better decisions made at local level.

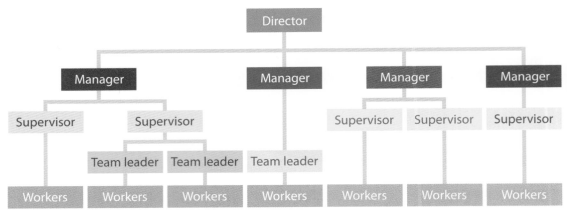

Family tree organisation chart

- Most organisation structures are in layers, with the people at the top having more authority than those at the bottom.
- Some businesses have a vertical or tall structure. This means that there are many layers but few people in each layer. Communication up and down may be slow.
- Some businesses have a horizontal or flat structure. There are few layers and many people in each layer. Although this means that communication within a layer is generally good, this sort of structure can make decision making hard.
- Some businesses may decide to remove layers to become more efficient. This is called 'de-layering'.

Boost your grade

AO1 to AO2: organisational structures often have in-built inefficiencies because of the way a business has developed; for instance, growth may have left managers in charge of departments that are too large. To raise your grade from AO1 to AO2, relate this reasoning to the business example you are given to support your knowledge.

Test yourself

Match the definition on the right with the correct term on the left.

1	authority	diagram showing relationships in a business
2	centralisation	the number of people for whom a manager is responsible
3	decentralisation	the right to pass on authority to others
4	delegation	decisions made by a few people
5	manager	decisions spread throughout the organisation
6	organisational chart	those over whom someone else has power
7	span of control	decision-making power
8	subordinates	a person with authority

Topic 19
Functional areas

What the specification requires

You will need to know that businesses are often organised into functional areas. You should know what these key areas are responsible for, and how they interact with each other.

In brief

All businesses have to carry out a number of functions in order to operate efficiently, but these are not always divided neatly into functional areas. For example, much of what used to be administration work is now carried out by managers — sending their own email, for instance, rather than dictating a letter. You will need to be able to show that you understand that these functions are carried out by all businesses, but are not necessarily divided into areas. The functions are usually given as finance, human resources, marketing, production and administration.

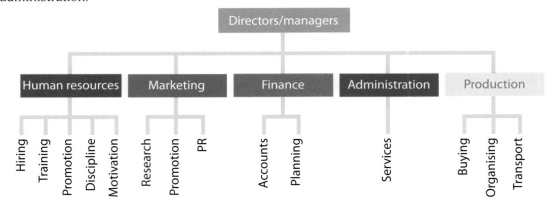

Functional areas in a medium to large business

Revision notes

Speak the language

budgets — financial limits set on processes, products, etc.

motivation — keeping people happy and wanting to work

reprographic — photocopying and similar jobs

- All businesses need to carry out these functions, but not always in separate departments. A sole trader, for instance, will carry out all the functions himself or herself.
- Finance deals with money and accounts. It manages the flows of money into, out of and inside the business. This includes setting **budgets**, paying wages, paying bills, etc. It also keeps all the financial records of the business. It must make sure they are accurate and available to any official body (e.g. tax authorities) that needs to see them.
- Human resources is in charge of all aspects to do with the people in the business. It hires people, trains them, promotes them if they do well, disciplines them if they break rules and releases them from employment. It deals with bodies such as trade unions and issues such as employment tribunals. It is also responsible for **motivation**.
- Marketing is in charge of three main areas linked to customers. It must find out what customers want, through market research. It must let customers know that products are available and where they can buy them, through advertising. It must try to persuade customers to buy the products of the business, through advertising and promotion.
- Production is linked to the actual manufacture of a good. Traditionally, it is in charge of buying and organising raw materials, buildings, machines and processes, and ensuring that all work together efficiently. It is also responsible for quality. Businesses that sell services will not have a production functional area, but will still have to maintain quality.
- Administration provides all the service operations that the business needs. This may include reception; communication; filing, **reprographic** and clerical work; organisation and record keeping (e.g. meetings and diaries); cleaning; and security.

In a nutshell

* Businesses need to be organised.
* There are various functions that must be carried out in any business.
* The main ones are finance, marketing, operations, administration, customer service and human resources.
* These may happen in separate departments.
* In smaller businesses, they will be carried out by owners.

Test yourself

State whether each of the following statements is true or false.

1 Administration provides all the service operations the business needs, such as cleaning and security.

2 The financial records of the business are kept by the administration function.

3 Advertising and promotion are part of the marketing function.

4 Budgets are set by the finance function.

5 Human resources deals with bodies such as trade unions.

6 Human resources is in charge of all aspects to do with the customers of the business.

7 In a small business, the owner will carry out all the functions himself or herself.

8 Marketing hires people, trains them and promotes them.

9 All businesses, whatever their size, need to carry out business functions.

10 Production is linked to the actual manufacture of a good.

AO1: if you think about what a business does, it will help you remember the functions. The business raises *finance* to produce a *product* that it will *market* to customers. For this it needs people (*human resources*) and paperwork (*administration*).

Topic 20

Why businesses change

What the specification requires

You will need to understand why businesses and their organisational structures change. You should be able to see why a business has changed, what it has changed, and what effect this might have on key stakeholders such as employees and customers.

In brief

Businesses can be very small or very large. They range from sole traders with no employees to very large concerns employing thousands of people. To get from one to the other requires growth and change. Changes may bring both benefits and drawbacks. For example, increased efficiency may be at the expense of employee motivation. Change comes about through growth, through changing product offerings or changes to a market.

Businesses can benefit from growth through economies of scale

Revision notes

■ A business can get bigger through either **internal growth** or **external growth**. Internal growth is also called organic growth. This is when the business grows larger from within, usually at a gradual pace, by increasing sales, using new technology, widening its product range to expand its markets, or winning a larger share of its main market. Changes that come about through internal growth are often slow and may therefore be easily managed.

■ External growth is when a business grows by joining with other businesses. It can merge with other businesses in an 'agreed marriage'. This is called a merger. Alternatively, it can take over another business in a hostile way. This is called a takeover.

■ Businesses can benefit from growth — for example, through **economies of scale**. These include the ability to buy in bulk, or save money on transport. There may also be problems with change. The business might suffer diseconomies, such as breakdowns in communication, or management being seen as far removed from workers.

■ Businesses may have to change as markets change. Products may become obsolete, or be replaced with newer, better products. Competitors may enter or leave markets. Flexible businesses plan for change and have policies in place to deal with it. This is called managing change.

■ Change may also occur through other changes to the marketing mix, such as changes in distribution methods. The use of internet retailing, for example, has made many businesses rethink the ways in which they reach customers.

In a nutshell

∗ Sometimes a business wants to grow.
∗ It can achieve growth internally (organically) or externally.
∗ External growth usually comes through merger or takeover.
∗ Mergers are 'agreed marriages'; takeovers tend to be hostile.
∗ Growth can bring benefits such as economies of scale.
∗ It can also bring problems such as breakdowns in communication.
∗ Not all businesses want to grow.

Speak the language

internal growth — (also called organic growth) growth from within the business

external growth — growth by combining with other business

economies of scale — cost benefits from growth

Test yourself

State whether each of the following statements is true or false.

1 A business can get bigger through either internal growth or external growth.

2 All businesses want to grow.

3 Internal growth is also called organic growth.

4 External growth is also called inorganic growth.

5 Businesses can grow through franchising.

6 Growing businesses do not get economies of scale.

7 Mergers are when two businesses agree to join.

8 Bulk buying is an economy of scale.

9 A royalty is a percentage of profits.

10 Takeovers are when two businesses agree to join.

Boost
your grade

AO1 to AO2: you will gain AO2 marks if you can relate the effects of a change, such as growth, to the various stakeholder groups of a business. Remember, while change may benefit some, others may lose out.

Topic 21

The effect of change on the workforce

What the specification requires

You will need to understand that patterns of work have changed, and continue to change. Businesses may have need of a more flexible workforce, with different skills, and a willingness to work different patterns such as part-time or under short-term or seasonal contracts. You should be able to weigh up the advantages and disadvantages of working from home for both the worker and the business.

In brief

Changes to businesses will affect their workforces. Changes may be made because the business needs to become more efficient, improve quality, or compete more effectively. Workforces can be changed permanently by employing more (or fewer) people, or temporarily, using contract workers, part-time workers or temporary staff. Freelance workers are used to achieve specific, often specialised, tasks.

Revision notes

- For a business to become more productive, either more workers must be brought in, or existing workers have to work harder or longer. The business may also change hours or times worked, type of job and even location.
- For the business to improve quality might mean new systems or different ways of working. It may mean training in new attitudes to quality.
- For the business to compete better may require new technology. Automation and **computerisation** of processes have removed many 'traditional' jobs, but new roles, connected with the new technology, have been created.
- Changes in both the products sold and distribution methods affect many employees. For example, many retailers now sell online as well as on the high street (a '**bricks and clicks**' operation). Sometimes the online element has become more important and retail premises have closed. Advantages to the business include not having to pay high rents and rates. Jobs such as call centre workers can even be moved abroad to keep costs down. Many UK call centres are now based in India.

Call centres can be moved abroad to keep costs down

- New technology also allows for more flexible working. It is possible for many workers to work from home. This could mean better use of their time, savings in travel, and freedom to organise work as they wish. On the other hand, they lose the benefits of **networking** (both socially and professionally), may lack specialist equipment and may be subject to distractions.
- For workers, these changes have meant more flexibility in some cases, and redundancy or less job security in others. Change is now such a force that workers no longer think of a 'job for life' but may take up several different jobs or careers during their working life. They will therefore need to keep retraining as part of a 'lifelong learning' culture (see Topic 13).

In a nutshell

* Changes are often made in businesses.
* Changes may seek greater efficiency, quality or competitiveness.
* These changes will affect businesses' workforces.
* Workforces can be changed permanently or temporarily.
* New technology allows for more flexible working.

Speak the language

computerisation — when processes are controlled by computers rather than people

'bricks and clicks' — a combined high street and internet retail operation

networking — meeting with other people and sharing ideas or experiences

Test yourself

Try this exam-style question.

Mobile phone technology and technology such as personal digital assistants (PDAs) even allow for working while on the move. Suggest what the advantages and disadvantages of this might be to:

(a) businesses

(b) workers *(6 marks)*

Boost your grade

AO2 to AO3: think about all the newest technologies available, such as video conferencing, Skype and internet ordering, and sites like YouTube and Facebook. To boost your grade from AO2 to AO3, you could suggest how these technologies could be of use to any business in both attracting and keeping customers, and cutting costs.

Topic 22

Communications in a business

What the specification requires

You will need to understand the methods, importance and effectiveness of internal and external communications in business, including the increased importance of information and communication technology (ICT) and its impact on business-to-business communications and communications with customers.

In brief

Clear communication is vital to all businesses. If the right message does not get to the right person, in the right format, then the business is failing to be efficient. Even worse, if the wrong messages are passed on, or in the wrong format, this could finish the business. ICT has brought about a number of changes in how businesses communicate both internally and externally.

Revision notes

- Any communication consists of five parts: the sender; the message; the **medium**; the receiver; and feedback from the receiver.
- Communications may be internal. These take place within the organisation, either horizontally between two people at the same level of an organisation, or vertically between different layers.
- Alternatively, communications may be external — with people or bodies outside the organisation.

Apple

The sender sends the message; the medium is text on the mobile phone; the feedback comes when the receiver responds and texts back

- The types of medium used will be both written and oral, and will include leaflets, catalogues, reports, press briefings, advertisements, formal documents, letters, meetings, emails and even texts.
- **Formal communications** have a set format and will be used for certain types of message. Examples are a formal letter of appointment or the agenda for a formal business meeting such as the **AGM**. There is usually a set format (e.g. the layout of a business letter) and a record of the communication will be kept (e.g. the minutes of a meeting). The main types of formal documents are reports, letters, memoranda (usually referred to as 'memos') and pre-printed forms. Some face-to-face or oral communications will also take place according to a set format — these include interviews, meetings, staff reviews and disciplinary actions.
- **Informal communications** can take place at any time, using any medium. Sometimes these can be more powerful than formal communications.
- ICT is vital to business. It is used for all types of communication. Internally, many communications are via email. Externally, ICT is used at the point where a customer comes into contact with a business. This ranges from the use of barcode scanners and itemised bills at checkouts to personalised texts, emails and mailshots. ICT also provides the business with records of what customers have bought and can even update stock. It can improve customer service and provide extra services such as online ordering and text updates.

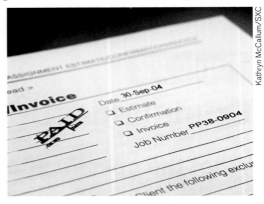

Documents are for formal communication

In a nutshell

* Clear communication is vital to all businesses.
* The right message must get to the right person, in the right format.
* The medium and message must be appropriate to sender and receiver.
* Communication channels can be formal or informal.
* ICT has changed the way that businesses communicate both internally and externally.

Speak the language

media — (singular, 'medium'); all the ways by which messages can be passed on, usually referring to either journalism or advertising

formal communications — take place according to set rules

AGM — annual general meeting; the official meeting of all shareholders in a limited company that must take place each year

informal communications — happen at any time and in any place

Boost your grade   **AO1 to AO2:** remember that informal communication channels can often be much more powerful than formal ones. Try to come up with an example from the business you are studying.

Test yourself

Fill in the missing words using the list below. If you are feeling confident, cover the words and do the exercise from memory.

.... communications take place within a business. .... communications are between businesses and other groups. They may be in a set format, called .... communications, or can take place outside a framework, called .... communications. The main parts of a communication are the ...., who sends the message through a particular way, or ...., and the .... An important part of the process is the receiver providing .... to show the message is understood.

external   feedback   formal   informal

internal   medium   receiver   sender

Section test: Business organisation

Read the passage and answer the questions that follow.

Barrowfell Sports Centre is part of a chain of sports centres called Fitness Max. It has sporting facilities, a pool and a café area. The manager, Paul, and his assistant, Asif, are full time. Personal trainers, pool staff and reception and café staff are part time. All staff receive basic health and safety training. Paul was appointed internally, having been assistant manager.

1   Which THREE of these statements, which refer to business organisation, are true?
  (a) An organisation chart shows how a business is organised.
  (b) Staff discipline is one of the functional areas.
  (c) In a decentralised organisation, decisions are made by a few people.
  (d) Most managers have few subordinates.
  (e) A manager is a person with authority.   *(3 marks)*

2   Use the organisation chart to answer the questions.

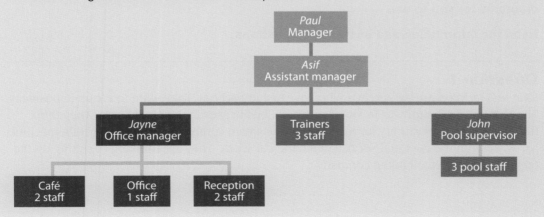

(a) What is Jayne's span of control?

(b) Identify Paul's immediate subordinate.

(c) Whom does John have authority over? *(3 marks)*

3 Fitness Max is divided into functional areas. State and explain what areas each of the following would cover.

(a) Finance

(b) Human resources

(c) Marketing *(6 marks)*

4 Fitness Max has grown into a large organisation, with economies and diseconomies of scale. State and explain one likely:

(a) economy of scale

(b) diseconomy of scale *(4 marks)*

5 Since the business has grown, new technology allows some administrative staff to work from home. Explain one advantage and one disadvantage of flexible working for the worker. *(4 marks)*

Total: 20 marks

Practice exam

The paper is marked out of 60 and you have 1 hour in which to complete it. Remember that papers will not cover the whole of the content, but will choose to concentrate on different content each year. The paper has some items and diagrams for you to use.

Read the information and answer the questions.

Question 1

John and Jackson are two friends who have just left school. They want to set up in business. They have seen the growth in 'hand car wash' businesses in their local area. They think that there is an opportunity for a better service which combines the efficiency of a machine car wash with the personal service of a hand car wash. They are thinking of setting up the business as a private limited company.

(a) **The following sentences each have a word or phrase missing. Choose from the list provided to complete each sentence.**

The opportunity the friends have seen is called a ....

Limited companies have limited ....

A company has a separate .... existence.

gap in the market   partnership   market map   liability   legal   marginal

(3 marks)

(b) **John and Jackson could also set up as a partnership. Explain THREE benefits of this form of organisation.**
(6 marks)

(c) **Explain TWO reasons why the friends might want to start a business.**   *(4 marks)*

(d) **Suggest and explain THREE factors that would be important when choosing the location of this business.**
(6 marks)

(e) **John and Jackson cannot decide between a partnership or a private limited company. Which form of organisation would you recommend to them? Give reasons for your answer.**
(6 marks)

Total for question 1: 25 marks

Question 2

John and Jackson think that they will not be able to staff the business themselves but will need some employees to help them in the business. They want to employ part-time staff to work at the busiest periods, as they think they can cope with demand themselves at other times. They know that they will have to follow the laws on recruitment and selection, particularly with regard to discrimination.

(a) **List THREE different ways in which John and Jackson could advertise for staff.**
(3 marks)

(b) **Explain the main factors that would make a job advertisement a success.**
(6 marks)

(c) **Explain why government legislation on discrimination is important when recruiting staff.**
(6 marks)

Total for question 2: 15 marks

Question 3

Megawash is a nationwide chain of car wash centres that operates by selling franchises. It has 20 sites of its own, plus 20 franchised sites. Each franchise pays 15% of its turnover as a royalty to Megawash. Indira Patel, its managing director, says its main objective is further growth and expansion. The organisation chart for Megawash is shown overleaf.

(a) **Which TWO of the following are benefits of growth? (i) Bigger market share, (ii) possible economies of scale, (iii) more competition, (iv) less choice for consumers.** *(2 marks)*

(b) **Explain what is meant by the term 'royalty'.** *(2 marks)*

(c) **Calculate how much a franchise with a turnover of £8,000 per year would pay to Megawash in royalties. Show your working.** *(2 marks)*

(d) **Use the organisation chart for this question.**
  (i) **What is Indira's span of control?** *(1 mark)*
  (ii) **How many subordinates does the finance director have?** *(1 mark)*
  (iii) **Explain what is meant by 'authority' using an example from Megawash.** *(2 marks)*

(e) **Explain why expansion may be an appropriate objective for this business.** *(2 marks)*

(f) **Explain TWO ways by which the business could grow, other than franchising.** *(4 marks)*

(g) **Recommend to Indira which method of expansion you think would be best for Megawash. Give reasons for your answer.** *(4 marks)*

Total for question 3: 20 marks

Overall total: 60 marks

Check your answers online at:
www.hodderplus.co.uk/philipallan

GCSE Revision Guide

Unit A293
Production, finance and external influences on business

Topic 23

Methods of production

What the specification requires

You should understand that different methods of production will be used when making a product or providing a service. You should be able to describe job, batch and flow production methods, and to explain when each would be appropriate. You should also know that businesses need to operate as efficiently as possible, and new technology may help them to do so.

In brief

Production describes the methods by which raw materials and other inputs are turned into outputs — and eventually into the final product. The method of production will depend on the nature of the product and the nature of the customer. Services are almost always produced to individual standards for individual customers — for example, you can only wear your own haircut! For goods, some will be produced individually, others in larger amounts and in standard sizes or shapes.

Hairdressing is an example of job production, as every customer has individual requirements

Revision notes

- Production describes the process whereby inputs are turned, via **transformation**, into outputs: for example, metal and components via manufacture into cars; and flour and water via baking into bread. The main methods of production are job, batch and flow. Job and batch production tend to be found in small businesses.

- **Job production** is where a product is a 'one-off' made to individual specifications: for example, made-to-measure clothes, a fitted kitchen or a customised car. This tends to be the most labour-intensive production method, and can lead to expensive outputs due to the craft skills that are usually needed for such products. Almost all services are individually tailored in this way.

- **Batch production** is where the same machinery and labour is used to produce different batches or groups of products. Batch production will take place in any manufacturing process where different sizes or colours are needed. For example, the same dress may be produced in sizes from 8 to 16; the same car, in different colours.

- Larger businesses will be able to use **flow production**. This involves a product being assembled or processed as it moves along a production line. Examples are car manufacture (production line) and oil refining (processing).

- The type of flow production where transformation involves a process (e.g. baking, refining, mixing) is sometimes called **process production**.

Speak the language

transformation — where a set of inputs, such as raw materials, is turned into outputs, such as finished goods

job production — when just one of a product is produced, using skills

batch production — producing different groups of a core product from similar inputs

flow production — a product being assembled, processed or built as it moves along a production line

process production — where a product is made through a process, such as refining or baking

division of labour — dividing work (and workers) up to specialise on a particular task

specialisation — when a worker concentrates on a particular task

The same model of car produced in different colours is an example of batch production

Fotolia

- Flow production allows **division of labour** to be used. Each worker can specialise in a particular task. This makes workers more efficient. It may also demotivate them through boredom.
- Flow production allows modern businesses to use **specialisation** and automation. Some processes can even be carried out by robots.

In a nutshell

* Production describes how inputs are turned into products.
* Small businesses mostly use job and batch production.
* Job production is used for 'one-off' products.
* Batch production uses the same inputs to make different versions of a product.
* Most services are 'job' produced.
* Larger businesses can use flow production.
* This lets them benefit from specialisation and division of labour.

Test yourself

Fill in the missing words using the list below. If you are feeling confident, cover the words and do the exercise from memory.

Batch production is where the same .... and .... can be used to produce different groups of products. Batch production will take place in any manufacturing process where variations to a basic model are needed, such as different .... or .... is where a product is a 'one-off' made to .... specifications, for example ...., a fitted kitchen or customised car. This tends to be the most .... production method, and can lead to .... outputs due to the craft skills that are usually needed for such products. Almost all .... are provided in this way. .... is used by large businesses to ...., often using a production line.

Boost your grade

AO1 to AO2: one main difference between job, batch and flow production is that bigger businesses can use flow production and gain the benefits of these. To earn AO2 marks, therefore, you must make sure that your answers are appropriate to the business that you are given.

colours   expensive   individual   job production   labour   labour-intensive

machinery   made-to-measure clothes   services   sizes   flow production   mass produce

Topic 24

Understanding added value

What the specification requires

You need to recognise that a successful business understands its competitors and knows about their strengths and weaknesses. This allows it to compete effectively by offering a **unique selling point** or by providing better value for money than its rivals. Successful businesses know how to add value. Value is added at each stage of the production process.

In brief

Businesses have to compete with other businesses for customers. Customers usually have a choice and will buy from the business that offers them the best value for money. Products will be designed to have unique selling points, to appeal to the target market by offering greater value than those of rivals. Businesses can add value in a number of ways. One way is through the production process.

Revision notes

- All businesses operate in markets where they will face some form of competition. Sometimes this is obvious, such as two butcher's shops in a village, or two rival car manufacturers. These are in direct competition with each other.

- Sometimes competition is less obvious. There may be just one butcher's in the village, but this is competing with butchers in other villages, supermarkets and even the internet! It is also competing with all those products that could be eaten instead of meat. The car manufacturer is competing not only with other manufacturers but with public transport, bicycles and the choice of staying at home.

- Customers always have a choice — they can always choose to go without the product that the business is selling.

- Businesses can compete by **adding value** to a product. This means making sure customers receive, or think that they receive,

Fotolia

A butcher's shop could be competing with other butchers or the local supermarket

better value for money than from a competitor. Common ways to add value are good service, convenience, providing ways to pay, speed and efficiency, and design features. Brands are also used to indicate added value.

■ The production process adds value at each stage. Once raw materials are turned into components they are worth more than previously. Once the parts are assembled into finished goods, these are again worth more. The addition of services, such as retail, convenience and delivery, adds further value. The final cost of a product is the sum total of all the values added at each stage of production.

In a nutshell

* Businesses are all in competition.
* Customers can choose which businesses to buy from.
* Businesses can compete by adding value to a product.
* Businesses can add value in a number of ways during the production process.
* They can also add value at the end of the process, through providing services.
* Added value will attract customers to a business instead of a competitor.

Test yourself

Choose the most appropriate answer from each of following alternatives.

1 New businesses need to analyse the strengths and weaknesses of competitors because **(a)** they need to employ people, **(b)** they will be able to compete more effectively, **(c)** they are on the high street, **(d)** they have internet access.

2 Adding value to a product means that a customer receives **(a)** competitor value, **(b)** more value for money, **(c)** more products, **(d)** better service.

3 The factor that makes your business stand out is called **(a)** the unique sticking point, **(b)** the unique sticking place, **(c)** the unique selling point, **(d)** the unique selling place.

4 Businesses can add value through all of the following EXCEPT **(a)** increasing price, **(b)** the production process, **(c)** increasing product range, **(d)** providing ways to pay.

5 Brands may be used to indicate which one of the following to customers? **(a)** Better service, **(b)** better products, **(c)** added competition, **(d)** added value.

Boost your grade

AO1: you can often access basic marks just by using the knowledge you have from your own experience. Think about the final price you paid for a good recently. Then list all the inputs that have gone into it. Where do you think the greatest value was added? Was it at the design stage? Is it the brand name? Was it at the final, retail stage? This will help you to explain value added.

Topic 25

The changing nature of technology

What the specification requires

You need to know that technology is constantly changing and that this has an impact on both what is produced and how it is produced. You should be able to talk about how changes have affected products (and productive efficiency), workers and customers.

In brief

New technology allows for more efficient production, but may need a better-trained and more flexible workforce. There are advantages and disadvantages to **specialisation** and **division of labour**. Workers can be very good at a specific task, but can also be bored and deskilled and lose interest in their work. Production can also be made more efficient through the use of lean production techniques, but staff may struggle with them if they are put under pressure. There are therefore implications for training staff and keeping them motivated. Technology also helps businesses to improve their offering to customers.

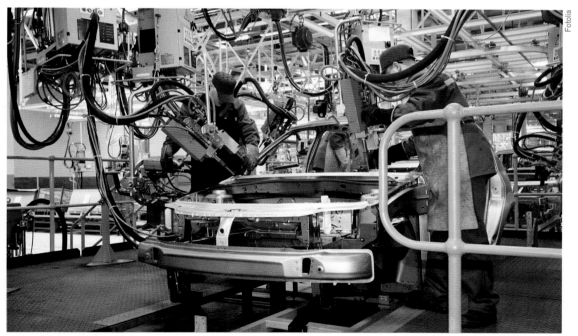

Machines can be used efficiently on a production line

Revision notes

- Businesses may be able to lower costs, using changes in technology such as computers.
- **Lean production** is the idea of being more efficient by minimising the use of all the inputs necessary for production. A business can cut down on all inputs but, perhaps most importantly, on time.
- The main version of lean production is the **just-in-time** (JIT) approach. Parts, components and other materials arrive just as they are needed. There is therefore no need for stock to be held, or for a business to bear the costs of storage. Of course, this means that an efficient distribution system is essential. If stock or parts do not arrive in time, the whole process is stopped. New technology can help to track parts and components and ensure that JIT systems work.

> ## Speak the language
>
> **specialisation** — when a worker is used for a specific job, so becomes highly skilled at it
>
> **division of labour** — dividing the workforce into small units to tackle small parts of a job
>
> **lean production** — minimising the use of all the inputs necessary for production
>
> **just-in-time** — a version of lean production where materials, components, etc. arrive just as they are needed

- Working to tight deadlines can be difficult and mistakes can be made. Working under pressure could demotivate staff. Employees are also a resource, so may need to be more flexible, as they may be needed only at particular times.
- Workers need proper training to cope with systems and this adds to the costs of the business.
- New technology also affects the marketing mix. It affects the range of products available and how these are both marketed (promotion) and delivered (place) to customers. For example, products can be customised, ordered online and delivered to customers. Promotions can be carefully targeted using new media such as texting.

In a nutshell

- * Businesses can increase efficiency, and reduce their costs, using new technology.
- * This can bring advantages to customers.
- * It can also improve productive efficiency.
- * New technology can also have drawbacks for workers.
- * Large businesses can also use lean production techniques.
- * There are implications for staff motivation and training when such systems are used.

Test yourself

Choose the most appropriate answer from each of following alternatives.

1 The production method when parts etc. arrive only as they are needed is called **(a)** test-in-time, **(b)** just-in-time, **(c)** batch production, **(d)** mean production.

2 Production that cuts down on the use of workers but can use more machinery is called **(a)** job production, **(b)** flow production, **(c)** batch production, **(d)** lean production.

3 Producing large quantities of a product on a production line is called **(a)** job production, **(b)** flow production, **(c)** batch production, **(d)** lean production.

4 Division of labour allows which of the following to be used? **(a)** Specialisation, **(b)** delegation, **(c)** job production, **(d)** induction.

5 Efficient production using the minimum number of inputs is called **(a)** job production, **(b)** flow production, **(c)** batch production, **(d)** lean production.

Boost *your grade*

AO1 to AO2: to reach AO2 marks you should be able to explain how technology may have impacted on the case study business. You must make sure that any suggestions are relevant to this business.

Topic 26
Maintaining quality

What the specification requires

You need to understand that businesses may face certain quality issues such as ensuring consistent quality of production. You should be aware of the costs of maintaining quality. You should know about the main ways of maintaining quality and how these may be applied to the case study business.

In brief

An expanding business may find that it is producing more of a product, or different products, as it moves into new markets. In either case, it must be careful to maintain the quality

Checking quality can be costly, but it is important for a firm's reputation

of its product by ensuring that processes are quality controlled. There are various techniques for doing this, both internally and using outside agencies or inspectors. There are costs to maintaining quality, but also costs in terms of lost reputation and falling demand if quality is not maintained.

Revision notes

- Growing businesses may face quality problems as production expands.
- A **quality** good or service is one that does what it is supposed to do. In UK law, it is fit for purpose. If the product does not do what it should, then the consumer has the right to demand his or her money back.
- Traditional quality control systems check that the finished product has reached the required standard. External inspectors can be used, but this involves a cost. The business must weigh up this cost against possible lost sales from not maintaining quality.
- TQM stands for **total quality management**. This system was first developed in Japan. The idea is that every single person involved in production is responsible for quality. Each worker (and each machine) checks for quality as the product enters an area, as it is processed, and before it leaves. The 'total' aspect also extends to parts, materials and other inputs. A truly TQM business will only deal with other TQM businesses.

- Another Japanese idea linked to quality is **kaizen**. This means 'continuous improvement' and states that it is every worker's job to see how his or her process could be made more efficient (however small that change). In this way, many small changes lead to improvements in quality and efficiency.
- There are international standards of quality that businesses can earn. These show other businesses (and customers) that this business is keen to maintain quality. One of the most important is ISO 9001, an international standard that has to be renewed each year.
- The **Kitemark**, in the UK, is used to show that products have passed quality tests set by the British Standards Institute (BSI).

In a nutshell

- To succeed, businesses have to produce quality products.
- Traditional quality systems involve checking products once finished.
- Some systems check all the way through a process as this finds problems earlier.
- A business concerned with quality will always be looking to improve it.

Test yourself

Try this exam-type question.

Xavier Clothing is a sportswear business, specialising in manufacturing kit for football, hockey, rugby and other team sports. It also sells a number of ranges of basic school PE kit.

Suggest and explain how a TQM system could be better than quality checks on finished clothing.

(6 marks)

Topic 27

Business costs

What the specification requires

You need to understand that businesses use a range of financial techniques to try to forecast sales revenues and costs, and from these, possible profits or losses. You need to know the different types of cost and to be able to work out simple costs for a given business.

In brief

Businesses produce either a good or a service for sale. If it is a good, then there are raw materials and other inputs to pay for. If it is a service, at the very least the business needs to let people know that it exists. In either case, therefore, there are costs. The money that the business receives for its sales is called **revenue**. Business costs are divided into **fixed costs**, also called indirect costs or overheads, and **variable costs**.

Revision notes

■ New businesses face 'start-up' costs that are paid once, when the business begins (e.g. the purchase of a computer for an internet business).

Daniel McCollum/SXC

A café needs to buy tables and chairs, crockery and cutlery, as well as stock, before it can start trading. It then has to pay for power, wages, cleaning and more stock to stay operational

These are also called 'sunk' costs. Once the business is open, there will be operating costs. These are the costs that have to be met for the business to keep operating and that have to be continually paid. They are sometimes called running costs.

- Costs may be fixed or variable. Fixed costs do not vary with output. Examples are rent, interest payments and rates. They are paid whether or not a business is producing.
- Variable costs vary directly with output. Examples are wages, raw materials, packaging, components, ingredients and power. Total variable cost (TVC) is calculated as quantity sold × variable cost per unit.
- Total cost (TC) is total fixed cost plus total variable cost.
- **Average cost** is the cost for each unit of production made by a business. It is worked out by taking total cost (TC) and dividing it by the number of items produced. As production increases, fixed costs are spread more thinly, so average cost will fall. This is an economy of scale (see Topic 28).
- Average cost is linked to price. To be profitable, the business must charge enough to cover its average costs.
- A business must try to keep control of its costs. Lower costs mean either that lower prices are profitable, so the business is better able to compete, or that the same price produces higher levels of profit.
- Businesses can reduce costs by buying materials or other inputs (e.g. labour) more cheaply. This would affect quality. Alternatively, it could increase efficiency or productivity.

Speak the language

revenue — the income of the business from sales

fixed costs — those costs that do not vary with production, like rent

variable costs — those costs that do vary with production, like raw materials

average cost — the cost for each unit of production made by a business

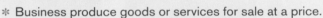

In a nutshell

* Business produce goods or services for sale at a price.
* There are costs involved in production.
* Costs can be listed in many different ways.
* Some costs are start-up or sunk costs; others are running, operating costs.
* Fixed costs do not vary with production; variable costs do.
* Average cost shows how much each product costs to produce.
* Price is often closely linked to average cost.

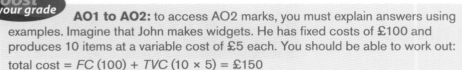

Boost your grade   **AO1 to AO2:** to access AO2 marks, you must explain answers using examples. Imagine that John makes widgets. He has fixed costs of £100 and produces 10 items at a variable cost of £5 each. You should be able to work out:

total cost = FC (100) + TVC (10 × 5) = £150

average cost = TC/quantity produced or 150/10 = £15

John must therefore charge a price of at least £15 a widget. You can then compare this with other businesses to see if he can compete.

GCSE Revision Guide

Test yourself

Try this exam-style question.

Stowford's makes just one type of rechargeable battery. Its fixed costs are £10,000 per year. Variable cost is £2 per battery and the firm produces 8,000 batteries in a year. It has two major competitors: one, Bindacell, charges £3.50 per battery and the other, Renewabubble, charges £4 per battery.

Calculate a competitive price from the above information. Explain why the price you have chosen is appropriate and competitive.

(8 marks)

Topic 28

Economies and diseconomies of scale

What the specification requires

As a business gets bigger, it is able to benefit from cost advantages over its smaller competitors. It can improve the **productivity** of workers, systems, or machines. Many of these advantages are called **economies of scale**. There are also disadvantages to growth, such as longer chains of communication, more remote management and more complex production processes.

> **Speak the language**
>
> **productivity** — the efficiency of resources; more productivity means more product from the same inputs
>
> **economies of scale** — benefits gained from the growth of a business
>
> **bulk** — a large amount

In brief

Businesses that grow to a certain size can begin to benefit from economies of scale, such as by buying in **bulk**, using bigger and better machinery, and using specialist managers. Many of these are within the control of the business, so internal. There may also be disadvantages or diseconomies of scale, most of which are linked to communication or organisation; more complicated production processes may bring problems. Businesses can also gain from the growth of their own industry.

Buying paper in bulk can help a printing company to save costs

Revision notes

- When a business grows, it has the chance to gain the benefits of economies of scale. These are benefits that a business can gain by, for example, buying in bulk, or producing in larger numbers. Diseconomies are when the growth of the business causes problems.
- There may be internal economies of scale within the business. The main economies are:
  - financial — cost savings through lenders treating the business as lower risk
  - bulk buying — obtaining lower prices by buying inputs in large amounts
  - technical — the use of specialist machines and workers
- Bigger businesses can also spread risk over a larger output and over a greater variety of output, diversifying into other products and markets.
- There can also be disadvantages to growth. Managers may become less efficient and more remote from the business's operations, making them less effective. The management structure is likely to become more complex and therefore unwieldy. Lines of communication can become stretched and decision making less efficient. Workers may feel remote from the hub of the organisation. This can mean that they are less loyal than they are likely to be to a smaller business.
- Specialisation may also lead to industrial disputes if workers are bored or undervalued.
- External economies may arise from the growth of an industry. The business may be able to attract skilled labour and managers, and specialised ancillary businesses providing components, raw materials and services to the industry.

In a nutshell

* Businesses that grow big enough can benefit from economies of scale.
* Most of these are internal.
* There may also be diseconomies linked to growth.
* These include poor communication and more remote management.
* Businesses can also gain externally, from the growth of their industry.

Boost your grade

AO1 to AO2: economies of scale are, by definition, only available to big businesses, so to achieve AO2 marks you must make sure that the business you have been given is big enough to benefit from them.

Test yourself

Match the economies of scale on the left with the correct statement on the right.

1	bulk buying	arising from the growth of a business
2	external	cost savings through lenders treating the business as lower risk
3	financial	arising from the growth of an industry
4	internal	using specialist machines and workers
5	technical	lower prices by buying inputs in large amounts

Topic 29

Breakeven analysis

What the specification requires

You should understand how to calculate breakeven for a business and interpret it. You should know how breakeven analysis can be used as a tool by a business, and be able to use it yourself.

In brief

Businesses produce either a good or a service for sale. **Revenue** is the amount received for sales. **Breakeven** is where total costs equal total revenue. Changes in any cost, or in revenue from sales, will alter the breakeven point. Breakeven can be used as a tool to predict the effect of such changes.

Revision notes

- Breakeven is where total costs equal total revenue — there is neither profit nor loss.
- Breakeven can be simplified by assuming that the **fixed** and **variable costs** of a business, along with its revenues, can be accurately measured. This can then be shown on a table.

Units sold	Sales revenue (£)	Fixed costs (£)	Variable costs (£)	Total costs (£)
0	0	15	0	15
1	10	15	5	20
2	20	15	10	25
3	30	15	15	30
4	40	15	20	35
5	50	15	25	40

- This business is selling items priced at £10. Revenue is therefore this price multiplied by the number sold. Fixed costs are £15; variable costs are £5 per unit. The point where total cost is equal to total revenue is the breakeven point — sales of 3 units, as highlighted on the table above.
- This can also be shown in graph form (see overleaf). The point where the total cost line crosses the revenue line is breakeven. Fewer sales (red) mean a loss; more sales (yellow) mean a profit. The further away sales are from the breakeven point, the greater the profit or loss.

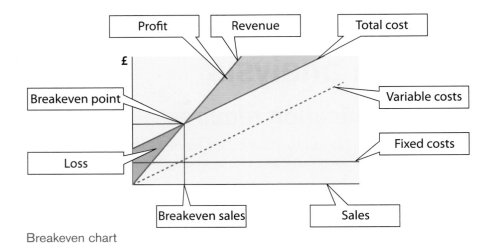

Breakeven chart

- To overcome the problems of inaccurate calculation using graphs, a formula can be used to work out the contribution of each sale towards breakeven. There are two parts to the formula:
  1 price per unit – variable cost per unit = contribution to fixed costs
  2 fixed costs/contribution = breakeven level of sales
- If a business is making a loss, it can try to make changes. It can lower costs or increase revenues. Managers can therefore use breakeven as a tool to help them predict what would happen as a result of changes. Breakeven is valuable to a business for 'what if?' scenarios to predict what would happen if factors like costs, revenues and sales changed.
- Businesses may want to ensure that they are not at, but above, breakeven, so that they are not in danger of making a loss. This is called the margin of safety.

In a nutshell

* Businesses produce goods or services for sale at a price and this involves costs.
* Costs can be listed in many different ways.
* When total cost equals total revenue, breakeven has been reached.
* Any change in cost or revenue affects breakeven.
* Breakeven can be used as a tool to predict 'what if?' scenarios.

Boost your grade

AO2 to AO3: to achieve AO3 marks, it is important that you not only work out breakeven from information you are given, but use this information to suggest changes or improvements to the business.

Test yourself

Copy the graph below and insert the correct labels (without looking at page 78).

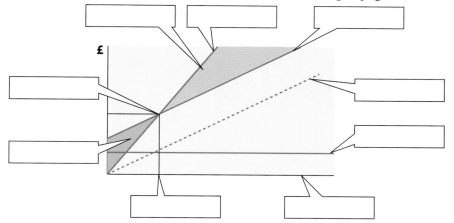

Section test: Using and managing resources

Read the passage and answer the questions.

Severin is a business that produces rugs. It makes 'designer' rugs to order for some clients and also sells a range of mass-produced rugs in its shop. The designer rugs are highly prized and carry the signature of the designer, Ziggy. The business has turned this into a logo which it prints on the back of all of its rugs. The owners see this as a unique selling point.

Recently the owners have been looking at the efficiency of production and are considering introducing a just-in-time system.

1   Define 'unique selling point'.   *(1 mark)*

2   Suggest TWO ways in which Severin could add value to compete more effectively. *(4 marks)*

3   Severin produces rugs by both job and batch production methods. Explain the
    main features of job production, with an example based on Severin.   *(3 marks)*

4   Define 'just-in-time system'.   *(1 mark)*

5   Suggest TWO possible disadvantages to employees of JIT and say how each
    problem might be solved.   *(4 marks)*

6   A typical batch of rugs is made with the following costs.
    Fixed costs: £1,000
    100 rugs produced at a variable cost of £50 each

    (a) Calculate the price that Severin must charge to break even.   *(6 marks)*
    (b) Calculate price with a 10% mark-up.   *(2 marks)*
    (c) Is this a competitive price? Give reasons for your answer.   *(4 marks)*

                                                                        Total 25 marks

Topic 30

Sources of finance: small and start-up businesses

What the specification requires

You should know that small businesses do not always find it easy to raise finance. You should be aware of the organisations that support new businesses, and the advice and support that is available. You should learn about the different sources of finance available to a small business, and be able to say when each would be appropriate.

Every business needs money

In brief

The money that a business needs may come from its owners, from lenders or people who are willing to take a risk, or from other outside sources. Small businesses will usually start with the owners' own funds as capital. They may also have some inputs from friends and family. Outside of this, it is usual to borrow money. Because small businesses might struggle, there are both government and charitable organisations that might help them.

Revision notes

- Small businesses may have difficulty raising the finance that they need.
- **Owners' funds** are one of the main sources of finance. It is the money that the owners already

have. Limited companies can raise funds by selling shares to the owners, who are the shareholders. Owners may also raise finance from friends and family, or from private investors called **venture capitalists**.

- A business may keep some profit for future finance. This is called **retained profit**.
- If business owners do not already have the funds, they will borrow. The most common forms of business borrowing are:
  - Trade credit — a business promises to pay later for goods received now (hopefully, after it has sold them).
  - **Overdrafts** — a bank allows the business to take more out of its account than it has deposited, up to an agreed limit. This is flexible and interest is only charged on what is actually owed.
  - Loans — a business borrows a fixed amount, for a fixed term, with regular repayments made and interest charged on the full amount for the term of the loan.
  - Hire purchase — paying a deposit and buying in instalments (e.g. a vehicle or machine).
  - Leasing — effectively, renting vehicles, equipment and plant.
  - Mortgages — long-term loans used to buy expensive items such as land or buildings, secured on the item bought.
- Business grants may also be available from sources such as the Prince's Trust.

> ### Speak the language
>
> **owners' funds** — the money that the owners already have
>
> **venture capitalists** — private investors willing to risk money on new businesses
>
> **retained profit** — profit kept by the business to help finance growth
>
> **overdraft** — bank permission to withdraw more from an account than is deposited

Sources of borrowing

Short term (from a few days up to 3 years)	Medium term (from 3 years to 10 years)	Long term (10 years +)
■ Overdrafts ■ Loans ■ Trade credit	■ Hire purchase ■ Loans ■ Debentures	■ Loans ■ Mortgages

In a nutshell

* Small businesses are often started with owners' funds.
* Other private sources of finance are also common.
* Otherwise, businesses will borrow from banks.
* The main forms of borrowing are overdrafts and loans.
* Government and charitable bodies provide support to business.

Boost your grade **AO1:** to access AO1 marks for knowledge, you must make sure that your knowledge is relevant. Although ventures capitalists are often in the news, they tend to back larger businesses, rather than small start-ups. So before using them as an example, check that they make sense in the context of the business you are using.

Test yourself

Fill in the missing words using the list below. If you are feeling confident, cover the words and do the exercise from memory.

The money which a business needs often comes from its .... This is called
.... Other finance will be raised from lenders such as .... It may also
come from profits kept back or .... Sometimes people with .... are
willing to take a risk on a business. These are called .... Small businesses may
also have .... from friends and family. Because small businesses might struggle,
there are both .... and charitable organisations that will help them. These include
the .... and charities like ....

banks   Business Start Up Scheme   capital   finance   government   owners

owners' funds   retained   the Prince's Trust   venture capitalists

Topic 31

Sources of finance: large and growing businesses

What the specification requires

Larger businesses may need different sources of finance as they grow. You should be able to recognise the advantages and disadvantages of each method of internal and external finance in a given situation. Two key considerations for a business are the amount of risk involved and the amount of control that has to be given up or shared.

In brief

A larger business can access different sources of finance. The main methods may be split into internal and external sources. **Internal sources** include retained profits and the sale of unwanted assets. **External sources** include share issues, becoming a public limited company or, as a plc, issuing more shares. Large businesses can also access larger loans, and are likely to have more assets, such as land and property, on which they can raise funds by using them as mortgage security.

Revision notes

- As a business grows, it may have more ways to raise finance than a smaller business. It is likely to have more **assets**, more profit and a better reputation than a small business, which may help it to raise finance from different sources.

Public limited companies can raise finance by selling shares via the stock exchange

- **Retained profit** is an important internal source of finance. Although it is a source for all businesses, a larger business may have more profit, and this is therefore a more realistic source of finance for larger than smaller businesses. Because retained profit is internal, interest does not have to be paid and the finance does not have to be repaid. The main disadvantage here may be to shareholders, who do not receive as high a share of the profit.
- A further internal source is the sale of unwanted assets. If a business has an asset that it no longer needs or uses, it can sell it off. For example, sales of redundant equipment might allow for the purchase of larger plant for increased production.
- Limited companies have access to finance through the sale of shares. A private limited company might decide to **'float'** on the stock market by inviting the public to buy shares and thus become a public limited company (plc). Plcs can also raise additional finance by selling more shares. However, each share gives the shareholder a right to part of the profit and to a say in how the business operates. This can make running the business difficult.
- External sources include the usual range of secured loans (e.g. mortgages) and unsecured loans available to business (i.e. increases in debt).

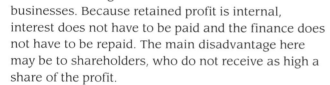

Speak the language

internal sources of finance — finance that comes from within the business

external sources of finance — finance that comes from outside the business

asset — something that a business owns

retained profit — profit that are not distributed to owners

floating a company — offering shares in the company to the public, via the stock exchange

In a nutshell

* Large businesses have more sources of finance that they can access.
* Internal sources include retained profits and the sale of assets.
* External sources include the sale of shares.
* Other sources, such as banks, may be persuaded to make larger loans to larger businesses, as a large business may have more security.

Test yourself

Choose the most appropriate answer from each of following alternatives.

1 A growing business is likely to have more of which of the following, to help it raise finance? **(a)** Products, **(b)** people, **(c)** assets, **(d)** liabilities.

2 Retained profit is what sort of finance? **(a)** Internal, **(b)** external, **(c)** long term, **(d)** short term.

3 Assets sales are what sort of finance? **(a)** Internal, **(b)** external, **(c)** long term, **(d)** short term.

4 Sales of shares on the stock market are what sort of finance? **(a)** Internal, **(b)** external, **(c)** long term, **(d)** short term.

5 Selling shares on the stock market is called which of the following? **(a)** Sinking a business, **(b)** floating a product, **(c)** sinking money into a company, **(d)** floating a company.

Boost your grade

AO1:
AO1 marks may be linked to the accuracy of your use of terms. You should therefore make sure that you know the difference between internal and external sources of finance for a large business.

Topic 32

Cash-flow forecasts

You need to understand the role and importance of cash to a business. You need to understand that cash flows into and out of a business, and these flows need to be managed. You need to know how a business uses cash-flow statements, to understand what cash-flow problems might arise and be able to suggest solutions.

In brief

A business has a constant flow of cash in and out. Cash comes in through sales revenue and flows out to pay for costs. Sometimes it takes the form of bank transfers, cheques, or credit or debit card transactions — but all are considered cash. A business needs enough cash to meet its day-to-day needs. The problem with cash is that the flows of it into and out of a business are never equal, so the business needs to manage these **cash flows**.

Revision notes

- Cash comes into a business from sales and other income; it leaves as a result of costs and expenses. If there is more cash coming in than the business needs, this is called a cash surplus. If there is less cash than it needs, this is called a cash shortage.

- A **cash-flow statement** shows past flows of cash into and out of a business. **Cash-flow forecasts** estimate future flows and help a business to predict when it will need to borrow extra cash. By forecasting cash inflows and outflows, a business can see where there might be shortfalls or excesses, and plan to even these out.

- Cash-flow forecasts can help the business see how to avoid problems. Techniques include spreading payments (e.g. making monthly payments rather than facing an annual bill) and arranging to receive revenue more regularly (e.g. getting customers to pay in instalments). Managing cash flow is linked with other issues: for example, cash could be tied up in stock, or be outstanding through sales made on credit. These issues are part of the management of cash flow.

Speak the language

cash flow — money flowing into and out of a business

cash-flow statement — flows that took place in the past

cash-flow forecast — a prediction of future flows

cash-flow crisis — when there is insufficient cash to pay immediate bills

Cash flows can be shown as either a graph or a table

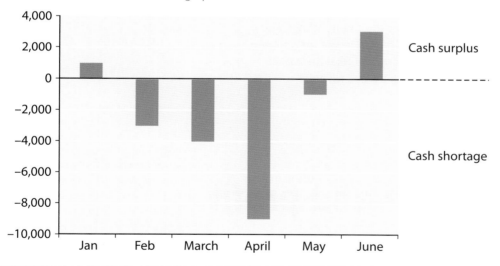

	Jan	Feb	March	April	May	June
Cash brought forward	1,000	1,000	−3,000	−4,000	−9,000	−1,000
+ Cash from sales	5,000	1,000	2,000	3,000	12,000	8,000
= Total cash available	6,000	2,000	−1,000	−1,000	3,000	7,000
− Cash out	5,000	5,000	3,000	8,000	4,000	4,000
= Cash to carry forward	1,000	−3,000	−4,000	−9,000	−1,000	3,000

- One of the major reasons why businesses fail is cash shortages. Even if a business has full order books and is making a profit, it cannot survive if it cannot pay its immediate bills. This is often called a **cash-flow crisis** and it can force a business into failure or insolvency. Having too much cash is also bad for business. Excess cash should be turned into assets that can earn more money.
- Writing a business plan reduces risk, as future problems can be forecast and managed.

In a nutshell

- ✳ Cash flows into and out of a business.
- ✳ These flows need to be managed.
- ✳ Too much cash is a waste of resources.
- ✳ Too little cash could lead to business failure.
- ✳ Businesses develop techniques to even out cash flows.

AO2 to AO3: with a topic such as cash flow, it is easy to reach AO2 marks by analysing figures. The cash position of a business is changed by a change in revenue or costs. You therefore have a range of possible methods to improve the position by reducing costs or increasing revenue. Remember, though, that most cost reductions have other effects on a business (e.g. cutting staff increases the workload for everyone else), and increases in price do not necessarily increase revenue.

Test yourself

Choose three different businesses: for example:
- a sole trader hairdresser business
- a limited company involved in manufacturing
- a plc supermarket chain

For each, say what are the main inflows and the main outflows of cash. Do not forget loans, whether personal or from banks, and other sources of cash besides sales revenue. *(6 marks)*

Topic 33

Revenue and profit

What the specification requires

You need to know that enterprise involves taking a risk — in order to gain a reward. The reward for a successful enterprise is the profit made by the business. You will need to be able to make simple calculations to work out amounts in a business. For example, you should be able to calculate revenue from price and sales information, and outcomes such as profit or loss from revenue and cost information.

In brief

To know how well a business is doing, it is necessary to calculate all of its costs and revenues. The difference between the two totals will tell you whether the business is making a profit or not. It is important to include all costs and revenues. Sometimes the cost of the owners' own time is not included and this gives a false picture of profitability.

Revision notes

- Entrepreneurs take the risk of starting a business. Their reward, if the business is successful, is profit. Business owners receive profit directly in simple organisations like sole traders and partnerships. They receive a share of the profit as part of a shareholding in a company.
- Profit is the surplus of income (revenue) over costs. Revenue is the income of the business. It is usually calculated as the number of products sold × the price of each product (good or service).
- Calculations of profit and loss are usually shown on a profit and loss account. Profit is said to be the reward for enterprise, or risk taking.
- **Gross profit** is calculated by taking the cost of sales (i.e. the cost of inputs such as raw materials, or parts, or stock) from total revenue. **Net profit** is calculated by then deducting **expenses** — running or operating costs such as power, labour, fuel, communications, loan interest, rent and rates (also called overheads).
- In a small business, it is important to make sure all costs (such as the sole trader's time) have been included in the calculations.
- Profits may mean that the business can expand. They signal to other businesses that this is a good market in which to compete. On the other hand, losses do not signal that a business is failing. It may take some time to grow revenue enough to make a profit, but losses may then be recouped. However, businesses that make long-term losses will be forced to close.
- Some businesses are set up with the intention of helping others rather than making a profit, or of sharing work and profit in a fair way. These are charities, co-operatives or other **social enterprises.**

easyJet

Entrepreneur Sir Stelios Haji-Ioannou is the founder of easyJet

Speak the language

gross profit — total revenue minus cost of sales

net profit — (also called operating profit) gross profit minus expenses

expenses — (also called overheads or operating costs) the day-to-day running costs of the business

social enterprise — an organisation set up to help groups or communities, rather than for profit

* price × number sold = revenue
* revenue − cost = profit (if positive), loss (if negative)
* gross profit = revenue − cost of sales
* net profit = gross profit − overheads
* It is essential to make sure all costs are included.

Test yourself

Calculate gross profit and net profit for each of the following.

1 Klippsta sells furniture. It buys £800 worth of timber and glue with which it makes 10 tables that sell at £200 each. Labour costs £200 and other overheads are £100.

2 Bigbuns the Baker's sells bread. It buys flour, salt, yeast and other ingredients for £140. It makes 150 loaves of bread, which it sells for £2.10 each. The gas used to heat the ovens costs £20 and the wages of the baker are £50. Other overheads are £100.

3 Burford's makes picture frames. It buys framing timber, glass, mounts and backing for £400. It makes 12 frames from these, of various sizes, that sell for a total of £650. Its overheads are £300.

(7 marks)

AO1 to AO2: when answering questions on accounts such as profit and loss accounts, AO1 marks are usually awarded for knowing how to work out various figures (e.g. net profit), while AO2 marks are given for analysing the figures. So you should be asking not just 'is this a good net profit?' but 'is it good for this type of business?'

Topic 34

Price and profit

What the specification requires

You need to know how a business might try to improve its profitability by changing price and therefore changing revenue. You need to recognise that a change in price does not always result in the change in revenue that was planned, and businesses must have good knowledge of their markets before they alter price.

In brief

Businesses try to break even (to make sure that costs are covered by **revenues**) and then to make a **profit**. Managers can try to increase profits by cutting costs or by increasing revenues.

The main way to increase revenues is through changes in price. Any action taken by a manager must be judged on its overall effect on the business, as there could be disadvantages to some actions.

Revision notes

- Price is often based on the 'cost-plus' model. This means that an amount for profit (called the **profit margin**) is added on to the total cost of a product.
- Profits can be increased by cutting costs, increasing revenue, or both. In trying to do any of these a business might bring about other consequences. For instance, cutting costs by cutting staff could leave remaining workers overworked and demotivated, and therefore less efficient. Cutting costs by cutting levels of stock might reduce storage and delivery charges, but leave the business with insufficient stock to be able to meet customer needs.
- Managers can try to increase revenue by raising or lowering prices. Increasing price will only increase revenue if sales either stay the same or do not fall by much as a result of the increase. If the increase in price leads to a large fall in sales, the business may actually suffer a fall in revenue. Sometimes a decrease in price is the way to increase revenue, as long as customers buy a lot more of the product as a result of the decrease.
- Businesses need to judge what will happen by knowing their market and estimating how their customers will react to a change in price. Market research is an important tool to show businesses how customers will react to a change in price.
- Managers can also try to increase the profitability of a business by making inputs or processes more efficient or productive.

Depending on customers' reaction, lower prices can either increase or decrease both revenue and profit

Speak the language

revenue — the income of a business from sales

profit — the excess of revenue over costs

profit margin — the additional sum added to cost to provide profit

In a nutshell

* Managers can try to improve the profitability of businesses.
* This can be achieved through lower costs or higher revenues.
* Changes in price will lead to changes in revenue.
* Managers need to think through the possible consequences of changes that they are planning, using their knowledge of the market.

Test yourself

State whether each of the following statements is true or false.

1 Profits can be increased by cutting costs or increasing revenues.

2 Paying workers a higher wage will lead to higher efficiency and profitability.

3 The profit margin is a measure that most businesses do not care about.

4 Breakeven is where revenues cover costs.

5 A lower price will always bring in more revenue.

6 A change in price will lead to a change in revenue.

7 The only way to increase profits is to cut costs.

8 Cutting back on the number of workers will always increase profits.

9 Increases in price will always lead to increases in revenue.

10 If an increase in price leads to a large fall in sales, revenue could fall.

AO2 to AO3: for AO3 marks you should be able to argue why a change may or may not work. For example, if you can explain why an increased price does not always bring about increased revenue, you will be working at AO3.

Section test: Financial information and decision making

Read the passage and answer the questions.

John and Jackson have seen the growth in 'hand car wash' businesses in their local area. They think that they can provide a better service, which combines the efficiency of a machine car wash with the personal service of a hand car wash. They have rented a site by a busy main road, where they intend to install a machine. There is an existing building where they will put a comfortable waiting area for customers to buy coffee, watch television and buy car care products. Cars will be cleaned inside, washed in the machine and then finished with hand polishing.

1 Outline the main costs and revenues for the business. *(4 marks)*

2 Explain TWO methods that John and Jackson might have used to finance their business start-up. *(4 marks)*

3 The car wash machine will cost around £15,000. John and Jackson have left themselves the choice of (a) borrowing £15,000 from Jackson's Dad, who would then want a shareholding, or (b) borrowing £15,000 in a 5-year bank loan, secured on the machine.

Discuss the advantages and disadvantages of each possible source. Recommend the best option. Give reasons for your answer. *(12 marks)*

Topic 35

Competition and monopoly

What the specification requires

You need to know what is meant by competition and monopoly, and the advantages and disadvantages of both types of market. You need to understand how monopolies are formed, and why governments might try to promote competition and prevent monopoly.

In brief

A market is anywhere that a business and its customers come together to decide on what to buy and sell, and the price to be paid. Some markets have many competing businesses; some have very few. This can bring advantages and disadvantages to both businesses and customers. The assumption is that competition will lead to lower prices and be better for the consumer, but this is not always the case.

Revision notes

- Different types of market exist for goods and services.
- These range from very competitive markets to markets with little or no competition. Very competitive markets have lots of businesses, sell a range of products and tend to have lower prices because of competition. Businesses in this market compete through customer service factors such as location and delivery, branding and advertising. Consumers have a choice of what to buy, and where from. Governments encourage competition because of these benefits.

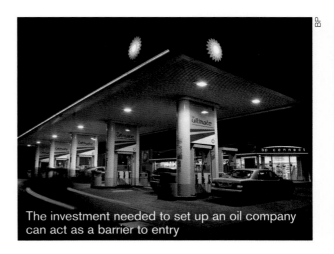

The investment needed to set up an oil company can act as a barrier to entry

- Monopolies are markets with just one major business and no significant competition. In the UK, if a business has a 25% market share, it is considered to be a monopoly. Often prices are held artificially high. Consumers have no choice but to buy from this business. However, the business may be able to afford to develop new products and **innovate**. It may also be able to offer low prices, because of economies of scale (see Topic 28).
- Monopolies can put up barriers to stop other businesses from entering their market. These **barriers to entry** include:
  - legal barriers — such as patents
  - supplier barriers — where the monopoly has contracts with the main supplier
  - high start-up costs — some industries require a lot of initial investment (e.g. oil)
  - marketing barriers — monopolies can afford to spend more on advertising and have strong brands
  - **restrictive practices** — such as agreeing price levels with suppliers or competitors
- Businesses may become monopolies through growing to be the biggest business in the market. They can take over other businesses. They can merge with competitors. The UK government has set up the Competition Commission to judge whether or not a merger or takeover is in the public interest.

In a nutshell

* There are many different types of market.
* They range from very competitive to monopolies.
* In a monopoly, one business dominates the market.
* It is usual to assume that competition is good for consumers.
* However, there are also benefits to monopolies, such as being able to develop new products.

Boost your grade

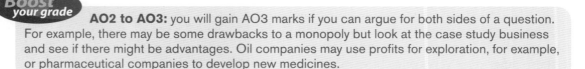

AO2 to AO3: you will gain AO3 marks if you can argue for both sides of a question. For example, there may be some drawbacks to a monopoly but look at the case study business and see if there might be advantages. Oil companies may use profits for exploration, for example, or pharmaceutical companies to develop new medicines.

Test yourself

Fill in the missing words using the list below. If you are feeling confident, cover the words and do the exercise from memory.

A .... is anywhere where a business and its customers come together to decide on what to buy and sell, and the .... to be paid. Very .... markets have lots of ...., sell a range of .... and tend to have lower ....

because of competition. .... encourage competition because of these benefits. Some markets have few businesses in them. .... are markets with just one major business and no significant competition. In the UK if a business has a ...., it is considered to be a monopoly. In these markets, prices may be .... and choice of product restricted. However, profits can be used for .... and innovation.

(25% market share) (businesses) (competitive) (development) (governments)

(high) (market) (monopolies) (price) (prices) (products)

Topic 36

Business and the environment: problems

What the specification requires

You should know how businesses and consumers can affect the environment — for example, through congestion, waste disposal and pollution. You should be aware of long-term environmental problems such as **resource depletion** and global warming. You should understand and be able to identify **social costs**.

In brief

All stakeholders have an interest in protecting the environment. It is where raw materials are taken from, where production — and living — take place, and where waste is disposed. All of these activities cause damage to the environment, some of which it may not be possible to reverse. The costs of environmental damage are shared by everyone.

Revision notes

■ The environment is where all stakeholders live, so it is in their interests to look after it as much as possible. Stakeholders benefit from the environment as a source of raw materials, a place to carry out business and a place to dispose of waste. It is also important as a place of leisure and relaxation, so striking a balance to keep the environment free from damage is important.

> **Speak the language**
>
> **social costs** — costs that affect the whole community, such as pollution
>
> **resource depletion** — using up limited resources
>
> **global warming** — the rise in global temperatures, believed to be caused by pollution, and the feared catastrophic consequences of this rise, such as the ice caps melting

Pollution is a major social cost created by businesses

- The main environmental problems created by businesses are resource depletion, pollution and waste products.
  - **Resource depletion** means that resources are being used up. There is, for example, a limited amount of oil left in the world.
  - Pollution can be air, water, noise, visual, even light pollution.
  - Waste has to be disposed of safely.
- These are costs that are carried by society as a whole (i.e. everybody suffers from them), so they are termed 'social costs'.
- Social benefits are gained and shared by everyone, but may also result in social costs. For example, faster deliveries may mean more road transport; better medicines lead to people living longer but add to population problems; internationally, a better environment at home may just mean that production has been moved abroad.
- Some costs, such as traffic congestion in the morning rush hour, may be short term and local. Others, such as increased carbon dioxide emissions from exhaust fumes and industrial processes, may be long term and lead to severe international problems such as **global warming**.

In a nutshell

* All stakeholders have an interest in protecting the environment.
* Stakeholders benefit from the environment as a source of raw materials, a place to carry out business and a place to dispose of waste.
* The main environmental problems created by businesses are resource depletion, pollution and waste products.
* Social costs are costs that are carried by society as a whole.

Test yourself

State whether each of the following statements is true or false.

1 Social benefits are gained and shared by everyone.

2 Waste disposal is not a problem for industry and society.

3 Oil is an example of a depleted resource.

4 Pollution can be air, water, noise, visual or light pollution.

5 Global warming is not a severe, long-term problem.

6 Traffic congestion is a short-term, local problem.

7 The increase in carbon dioxide levels is a short-term, local problem.

8 The environment is a source of raw materials.

9 Only a few stakeholders suffer if the environment is damaged.

10 Social benefits may also cause social costs.

AO1 to AO2: look at the ways in which a given business could be more environmentally friendly in areas such as waste, pollution and resource use. Make sure any comments are appropriate to the business that you use.

Topic 37
Business and the environment: solutions

What the specification requires

You should know how businesses, consumers and governments work to improve the environment, and can try to reduce or remove future problems. You should be able to discuss government solutions such as carbon permits, business solutions such as sustainable production and consumer solutions such as the use of less energy and renewable energy.

In brief

It is in the interests of businesses to reduce environmental problems. Environmental policies are often built into the aims and objectives of the business, to demonstrate what businesses call **corporate social responsibility** (CSR). Acting in an environmentally responsible way is often attractive to customers, so it helps to bring about customer loyalty. The UK government has also passed laws to make sure that businesses do not damage the environment or present a danger to communities.

Revision notes

- Many businesses aim to be environmentally responsible. This can bring advantages, including greater efficiency and lower costs. For example, more fuel-efficient vehicles are both better for the environment and cheaper to run; removing excess packaging is better for the environment but also cuts costs.
- There is also likely to be increased custom from having a better reputation. Being seen as **environmentally friendly** may be one of the main objectives of a business.
- Many businesses and consumers have recognised their impact on the local, national and international environment, and have taken steps to reduce this. The most common methods of reducing **carbon footprint** are:
  - recycling paper and packaging, and using recycled paper for packaging
  - only using timber from sustainable forests
  - fitting pollutant controls (e.g. smoke filters) wherever possible
  - using 'green' fuels in transport — usually meaning high performance in terms of miles per litre
  - fitting pollution reduction devices such as catalytic converters
  - energy-saving policies such as lighting systems that switch on and off only when areas are in use
- Many businesses also aim for **sustainable production** as, globally, resources decrease. This means ensuring that anything taken from the environment during production is replaced. They also plan to use more **renewable resources** and alternative technologies, such as wind and solar power.
- Governments use taxation and regulation to discourage energy waste and pollution. Examples include road tax and laws on car exhausts and factory waste. Carbon permits limit the amount of carbon that a factory may produce and so reduce carbon levels. Governments also encourage and support recycling and low-energy alternatives, such as 'green' lightbulbs.

Tesco

Tesco is aiming to reduce its carbon footprint by 50% by 2020 — transporting goods by train is one way to reduce its carbon dioxide emissions

Speak the language

corporate social responsibility — a business policy that covers environmental and ethical issues

environmentally friendly — not harming the environment

carbon footprint — the amount of carbon released (and therefore environmental damage caused) through an activity

sustainable production — ensuring that anything taken from the environment during production is replaced

renewable resources — those that can be replaced (e.g. a new tree can be planted for each one felled for timber)

In a nutshell

* Businesses should be friendly to the environment.
* An environmentally friendly approach is good for a business's reputation and customer loyalty.
* This means that it often also makes good business sense.
* Businesses can develop new technologies and less damaging alternatives.
* Governments encourage environmental policies and discourage pollution and waste.

Test yourself

Fill in the missing words using the list below. If you are feeling confident, cover the words and do the exercise from memory.

Businesses can bring both benefits and .... to the .... within which they operate. Although businesses may provide jobs, they may also cause ...., such as ....

Many businesses regulate themselves, to make sure that the bad effects of their business do not upset the .... Often they include environmental targets in their .... The advantages of being .... include greater .... and lower .... There is also increased custom due to having a better ....

Boost your grade

AO2 to AO3: you will gain more marks if you are clear that there are often dual benefits to being environmentally friendly. Policies may both reduce costs and increase customer loyalty. AO3 marks will be gained if you can recommend, with reasons, how a given business can reduce its impact on the environment.

communities   costs   disadvantages   efficiency   environmentally friendly   local community   objectives   pollution   reputation   social costs

Topic 38
Ethical issues affecting business

What the specification requires

You should understand the meaning of the term 'ethics' in business and why businesses are keen to be seen to be acting in an ethical manner. You should know that sometimes the ethical route is not the most profitable one, so this can cause conflict. You should be able to explain how customers can influence businesses by changing what they buy.

In brief

It is in the interests of businesses to have ethical policies. Such policies are often built into the aims and objectives of the business. Acting ethically means 'doing the right thing'. Examples include not testing products on animals, paying fair prices for materials and skills, not using cheap or child labour, and not carrying out production in dirty or dangerous conditions. Acting in an ethical way is often attractive to customers, so it helps to bring about customer loyalty.

Revision notes

- Businesses should act in **ethical** ways: that is, they should be moral in their actions. In practice, this means not harming the communities in which they produce and sell, and not taking advantage of weak laws. They should also pay fair prices and not exploit producers or labour.
- Businesses are often keen to act ethically, as a good reputation in this area increases customer loyalty and sales.
- An ethical approach may have an impact on profits: for example, paying a fair price for supplies may mean paying a higher price. However, in the longer term, increased costs may be recovered through better sales, as customers prefer to buy products that have been sourced and produced in an ethical manner.
- Many investors in businesses will only invest in those that have ethical policies. This is called **ethical investment**. Many customers change their buying habits away from businesses that are, or seem to be, unethical, and support those that are ethical.

The Cooperative Group's investment in fair trade products is an example of ethical trading

- **Pressure groups** are groups of people or organisations that try to influence businesses and governments to act in ethical ways (or what they consider to be ethical ways). Well-known pressure groups include the environmental group Greenpeace, the World Wide Fund for Nature, PETA (People for the Ethical Treatment of Animals) and many charities. Pressure groups often use publicity gained from stunts to get their message across.
- Pressure groups may also reveal when businesses are acting unethically. They have challenged many major companies by finding child or cheap labour used in production, dangerous working conditions, or other unethical practices.

Speak the language

ethical — acting in a moral way

ethical investment — only investing in those businesses that have ethical standards

pressure groups — organisations that campaign for particular causes or changes

In a nutshell

* Businesses should act in a moral — or ethical — way.
* This might impact on profitability.
* An ethical approach is good for a business's reputation and customer loyalty.
* An ethical approach may therefore be good for business.

Test yourself

Try this exam-style question.

Crossfell is a worldwide business, specialising in sports equipment, sports clothing and sports shoes. It has operations all around the globe, including the European Union, North and South America and Asia, especially the Far East.

Crossfell has a CSR policy that covers ethics and the environment. Crossfell's ethical image was damaged last year by problems with an advertising campaign. Its Zipfast range of shoes had a graffiti-like logo which Muslim commentators pointed out spelt out an insult in Arabic. Also, the advertisement for the Zipfast range claimed that the product would help customers to run faster and recover from effort more quickly. These were claims that the business was unable to back up.

Boost your grade

AO2 to AO3: analysing the advantages of being ethical is not difficult. You will earn AO3 marks if you can clearly say that all the good practice is also good for enhancing a business's reputation. You could also link ethical targets to ideas of growth, both in the developed and in the developing world.

1 Explain what is meant by CSR and 'ethical aims'. *(5 marks)*

2 Explain how Crossfell may have breached *its own policy* and recommend what action it should take. *(6 marks)*

3 Explain how the advertisement might be seen *by customers* as unethical and what action Crossfell should take. *(4 marks)*

Total: 15 marks

Business cycles

What the specification requires

You should know that economic activity tends to rise and fall in cycles, with periods of growth followed by periods of recession. You need to understand that businesses are affected by business cycles, and by changes in consumer incomes and employment levels, and therefore their pattern of spending.

In brief

Changes to the economy tend to happen in cycles that go from 'boom' to 'bust' via 'recovery' and 'recession'. Changes in economic activity are used to chart the cycles. When economic activity (i.e. production, employment and consumer demand) is on the increase, businesses find it easier to survive, succeed and become profitable. When economic activity is decreasing, many businesses will find it hard to survive and may only manage to do so by cutting back on costs, such as staff.

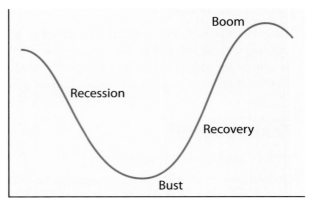

The business cycle

Revision notes

- **Economic activity** tends to go in cycles that are reckoned to last for between 8 and 10 years.
- Cycles go from years of 'boom' through downturns called **recessions** and then on to upturns or 'recovery'.
- Boom years have high levels of consumer spending and low levels of unemployment. However, at the top of the boom, there will be rising wages and rising prices. Businesses will find it harder and harder to meet increased demand, which is what pushes prices up.
- During a recession, consumer demand falls (as a result of higher prices and interest rates), and there is lower spending and high levels of unemployment. Businesses may find it harder to borrow money and this can be a particular problem for small businesses.

Speak the language

economic activity — the level of demand and output in the economy as a whole

recession — when growth is either zero or negative for a period of time

economic growth — increases in output and demand in the economy

- Levels of economic growth signal whether an economy is heading for boom or recession. **Economic growth** measures production and expenditure in an economy. Positive growth means strong demand. This is generally good for businesses.
- Negative or zero growth means weak demand. This is bad for businesses and many may struggle to survive.
- Small businesses are likely to be more vulnerable and the first to be badly affected by a recession. However, the effect on a business depends on the type of business. Those selling luxury products and services that people can easily do without, such as foreign travel and holidays, are likely to suffer most. Those selling necessities are likely to suffer least.

In a nutshell

* The economy goes through periods of growth and recession.
* This is measured through economic activity, such as demand.
* When demand is growing, businesses find it easier to do well.
* When demand falls, many small businesses find it hard to survive.
* Most likely to be affected are those businesses selling products that people can easily do without.

Boost your grade   **AO1 to AO2:** for basic marks you should be able to describe how a business might suffer in an economic downturn. You are not expected to know specific terms used in talking about business cycles, such as 'recession', but will gain AO2 marks if you can use them to show better understanding in the context of an answer.

Test yourself

1 Match the term or phrase on the left with the most appropriate term or phrase on the right.

(a)	boom	recession
(b)	bust	recovery
(c)	high unemployment	high consumer spending
(d)	rising wages and prices	bottom of a cycle
(e)	upturn	top of a cycle

2 Draw a business cycle diagram and label it correctly.

Section test: Business issues and influences

Read the passage and answer the questions.

Getafone is one of the newest competitors in the UK mobile phone market, but is rapidly taking market share because of its concerns for the environment. Mobile phones are made from many different materials, including zinc and aluminium, both of which are often mined under terrible working conditions. Getafone has ethical policies in place to make sure that none of the components of its phones come from such sources.

Getafone is a UK-based company that sells phones internationally. In its latest corporate social responsibility (CSR) report, Getafone has promised to reduce the carbon footprint per phone by at least 25% by 2015.

1 Complete the following sentences by choosing the most appropriate word from the list given.
   (a) Governments encourage .... because they think it will lead to lower prices.
   (b) .... can build barriers to stop other businesses from entering their markets.
   (c) .... are anywhere where a business and its customers come together to decide on what to buy and sell.

   (monopolies)   (governments)   (growth)   (competition)   (markets)

   (3 marks)

2 On which THREE of the following would you expect comments in a corporate social responsibility (CSR) report? (a) Policy, (b) energy-saving policies, (c) European Union policy, (d) ethical policies, (e) exchange rate policies, (f) sustainability policies. *(3 marks)*

3 The types of mobile phone sold by Getaphone are seen as being luxury items, so demand has fallen during the recession.
   (a) Outline TWO features of a recession. *(2 marks)*
   (b) Suggest and explain ONE action the UK government could take to improve Getaphone's situation. *(3 marks)*

4 (a) Explain what is meant by the term 'carbon footprint'. *(2 marks)*
   (b) Suggest and explain THREE ways by which Getaphone could reduce its carbon footprint. *(6 marks)*
   (c) Recommend which of the ways you have suggested in (b) would be best for this business. Give reasons for your recommendation. *(6 marks)*

Check your answers online at:
www.hodderplus.co.uk/philipallan

Total: 25 marks

The wider world

Topic 40

Government and its influence on demand

What the specification requires

You will need to understand how the UK economy can be affected by changes in demand for goods and services. You should be able to explain how government spending, taxation and interest rates affect demand, and therefore business. You should also be able to consider other **external factors**, such as population changes.

In brief

Businesses are affected by many external factors over which they have little or no control. These factors include the actions of central bodies such as the government and the Bank of England. Between them they influence demand through changes in taxation, government spending and interest rates. These changes can be accidental, but are more often a result of a deliberate policy to change the amount or pattern of demand in the economy, either to boost or to discourage spending and saving.

Revision notes

- Businesses are affected by changes in government spending, taxation and interest rates.
- **Interest rates** are the price of borrowing money. In the UK, they are set centrally, not by government, but by the Bank of England. If interest rates are high, or increase, this makes it more expensive to borrow money. This has an effect on both businesses and consumers.

- Businesses, particularly small ones that rely on overdrafts, bank loans and good credit terms with suppliers, will find it more expensive to borrow if interest rates rise. They may not be able to hold as much stock, or as wide a range as they would want to. They may also not be able to offer credit terms to customers. Higher interest rates also reduce consumer spending.
- Taxation can affect the ability of businesses to survive and compete. Taxes on consumers affect demand. An increase in income tax makes consumers worse off, so they may spend less. An increase in VAT makes the price of products higher. Governments can change taxation either to try to boost or dampen down demand. Taxes on business profit may also discourage businesses.
- Governments also spend on services such as education and major projects such as roads and hospitals. This can boost businesses and the economy.
- Population changes will also affect demand. The UK has an **ageing population**. This means that more people are living longer. This puts a strain on the health service and on pensions. The UK also has a history of welcoming people from other nations. These immigrants bring benefits such as increased demand, different skills and more diversified culture. They also bring costs in terms of education and the health service.

Speak the language

external factors — outside the control of the business

interest rates — the price of borrowing money

ageing population — where there are more older people in a population than younger ones, usually because people are living longer

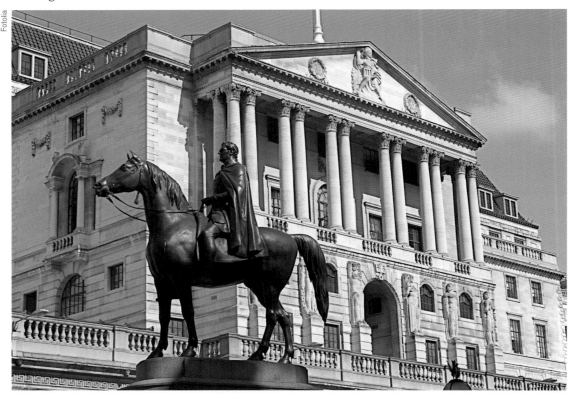

Fotolia

The Bank of England sets interest rates in the UK

In a nutshell

* Some influences are external — outside the control of the business.
* These include rates of interest, set by the Bank of England.
* One external influence is government.
* Government can change taxation and its own spending to influence demand.

Test yourself

Fill in the missing words using the list below. If you are feeling confident, cover the words and do the exercise from memory.

Businesses are affected by changes in .... These include ...., taxation and interest rates. .... are the price of borrowing money. They are set centrally in the UK, not by government, but by the .... High rates make it harder for businesses to .... Higher .... on consumers can cause .... to fall. An increase in .... will make consumers worse off, so they spend less. An increase in .... makes the price of products higher. Taxes on .... may also discourage businesses.

Bank of England   borrow   business profit

demand   external factors   government spending

income tax   interest rates   taxes   VAT

Topic 41
Globalisation

What the specification requires

You will need to know what is meant by the term 'globalisation', and how it has developed in recent years. You should be able to explain the possible advantages and disadvantages of globalisation to businesses and consumers in the UK. You should understand how the global picture is constantly changing, as countries like China and India become developed.

In brief

Globalisation describes the move by businesses towards operating on a worldwide basis. This leads to better and cheaper products, but means that businesses are increasingly dependent on each other. There are also problems associated with globalisation, as big businesses are able to exploit poorer countries and their workers.

Revision notes

- **Globalisation** describes how many businesses now operate on a global scale.
- Many companies which operate on a global basis are **multinationals**, with factories and other operations in many countries. This allows them to move investments and profits to keep costs and taxation low. They may also be able to take advantage of lower labour costs, or less organised labour. This has brought globalisation into conflict with human rights groups, which see global businesses as exploiting labour or natural resources in poorer countries in order to boost profits in richer ones. Some businesses are criticised for this. Others are congratulated for bringing work to poorer countries.
- **Global brands** have become increasingly important to big businesses. Such brands mean that the same good or service, with the same qualities and reputation, is available around the globe. Sometimes this may mean a name change, as in the case of the 'Marathon' bar, which became 'Snickers' in the UK to match its international name. More often than not global brands are linked to particular images or lifestyles. In the UK there are benefits and problems due to globalisation:

McDonald's

Global brands are recognised all over the world

- for consumers, who gain greater choice of products, often at lower prices, but may ultimately have less choice if one global brand destroys competition
- for businesses, who gain cheaper supplies and a larger market, but face more competition
- for employees, who can take jobs in global companies, but may be undercut by cheap labour abroad

■ Developing nations also want to compete globally and this can cause increased environmental problems. Countries such as China, India and Brazil have seen rapid economic growth. This has increased competition and lowered prices, but there are problems with the environment and areas such as health and safety, labour rights and child labour.

In a nutshell

* Many businesses now operate on a global basis.
* This has made businesses and industries much more dependent on each other.
* Businesses can gain from globalisation by taking advantage of local labour rates and laws.
* Consumers can gain through lower prices and greater choice.
* However, there are also problems, such as child labour.

Test yourself

State whether each of the following statements is true or false.

1 Consumers always benefit from globalisation.

2 Businesses that operate abroad face more competition.

3 China, Brazil and India are still undeveloped.

4 Some businesses take advantage of local labour rates in poor countries.

5 Globalisation can cause environmental problems.

6 Child labour is never used by global businesses.

7 Global brands are recognised all over the world.

8 Businesses always operate with the interests of local people at heart.

9 Multinationals operate in several countries.

10 Many businesses operate globally as well as locally.

Boost your grade

AO2 to AO3: if you can show that you are up to date in your knowledge, by mentioning how developments in countries like China, Brazil and India have increased globalisation, you will be earning AO3 marks.

External economic influences: exchange rates

What the specification requires

You need to understand that changes in exchange rates may be important for some businesses, depending on the nature of the market in which they operate. You will need to know how to calculate changes in exchange rates and the actions that businesses can take to reduce the effect of exchange rate changes.

In brief

Foreign exchange rates show the price of one currency in terms of another and are important to any business trading internationally. Changes in foreign exchange rates have an influence on many businesses, both small and large. The extent of the influence will be strongly linked to the type of market in which the business trades. Businesses can take steps to avoid the worst effects of exchange rate changes.

Without international trade, many of the products that we take for granted would not be available to us

Revision notes

- **Exchange rates** are the value of our currency (the pound sterling, £) in terms of other currencies (e.g. the US dollar, $, or the EU euro, €). Businesses trading internationally will have to buy or sell in a foreign currency. If a UK business imports a product from Europe, it will have to pay in euros, so at some point a pound-to-euro conversion takes place. The value of the pound will fluctuate depending on many factors, such as the strength of the economy and interest rates. A higher pound means cheaper imports and more expensive exports (and vice versa). For example, at an exchange rate of £1 = €2, a £100 export sells for €200. If the exchange rate falls to £1 = €1.5, a £100 export is now only worth €150.

- Almost all businesses are affected in some way by exchange rates. Even if they do not buy or sell their product abroad directly, they may receive supplies or parts from abroad, or face competition from businesses based abroad.

■ High exchange rates are a problem for businesses that **export**, as they cause the price to the buyer to increase. The business may need to reduce prices, or change the countries to which it exports.

■ Low exchange rates are a problem for businesses that **import**, as they cause the import price to increase. These businesses may need to pass price increases on to consumers, take reduced profits, or cease trading with particular countries.

■ Businesses can try to predict what will happen to a currency and buy or sell it in advance of the change. This is only of use if they get the prediction right!

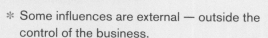
In a nutshell

* Some influences are external — outside the control of the business.
* One external influence is the price of other currencies — foreign exchange.
* Changes in foreign exchange rates can have an effect on a business that exports or imports.
* The size of the effect depends on the market in which the business operates.

Speak the language

exchange rates — the price of one currency in terms of another

export — sell products from one country to other countries

import — buy products from other countries

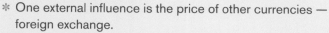
Boost your grade

AO1: you may be asked to do simple calculations with regard to exchange rates. You should always check these carefully, first, to make sure that you have gone in the right direction (dollar to pound, or pound to dollar, for example), and second, to make sure that you have the decimal point in the right place.

Test yourself

Calculate the price in US dollars, euros or sterling of each of the following, as appropriate. Assume that the exchange rates are £1 = €1.1 and £1 = $1.6.

1 A UK business buys £1,000 worth of fruit from France.
   (a) Will payment be made in dollars, pounds or euros?
   (b) What is the amount to pay?

2 An American car manufacturer sells £150,000 worth of cars to a garage in London.
   (a) Will the garage make payment in dollars, pounds or euros?
   (b) What is the amount to pay?

3 An Italian tourist buys a holiday in the Lake District in northern England. It is priced in Italy at €750.
   (a) Will payment to the holiday company be made in dollars, pounds or euros?
   (b) What is the amount to pay?

4 A UK business buys £20,000 worth of wheat from the USA.
  (a) Will payment be made in dollars, pounds or euros?
  (b) What is the amount to pay?

5 A German business needs payment for £3,000 worth of parts sold to a Birmingham car company.
  (a) Will payment be made in dollars, pounds or euros?
  (b) What is the amount to pay?

Topic 43

The European Union

What the specification requires

You need to know about the European Union and how it can both help and hinder UK business. You should be able to discuss the advantages and disadvantages of membership to both consumers and businesses. You should know about the euro and how this could help businesses.

In brief

The **European Union** (EU) is a group of countries in Europe which have agreed to act together on a number of issues, many of which affect business. This provides businesses within the EU with a larger market (the **single European market**) of over 500 million people. It has introduced common measurements and a common currency, both of which help business.

Revision notes

- The EU is a powerful **trading bloc** which other countries are keen to join. At the time of writing it has 27 member states and stretches from Sweden and Finland in the north to Malta and Greece in the south, from Portugal and Spain in the west to Romania and Bulgaria in the east. It allows free movement of goods and workers within its borders.

Speak the language

European Union — a 'club' of 27 member states that act and trade together

single European market — within EU borders, goods and labour are free to move as if there were no borders

trading bloc — countries that gain trading power by trading as one group

Social Chapter — the part of the Maastricht Treaty that dealt with issues such as workers' rights; countries could choose to bring in changes gradually

harmonisation — making things the same in all member countries

- The EU provides grants and subsidies to help businesses and poorer countries within it. European regional policy helps those regions where traditional industry has declined and where unemployment is high. Regional funding is also available to help develop transport and services. The European Social Fund pays for retraining workers and programmes to regenerate industry.

- The Maastricht Treaty of 1991 was designed to encourage all member states to work within the same rules. It included the **Social Chapter**, which promoted:
  - the right for workers to join a trade union
  - the right to equal treatment for men and women at work
  - more worker involvement in businesses through worker councils
  - a minimum wage
  - maximum working hours
  - freedom for EU citizens to work in any EU country

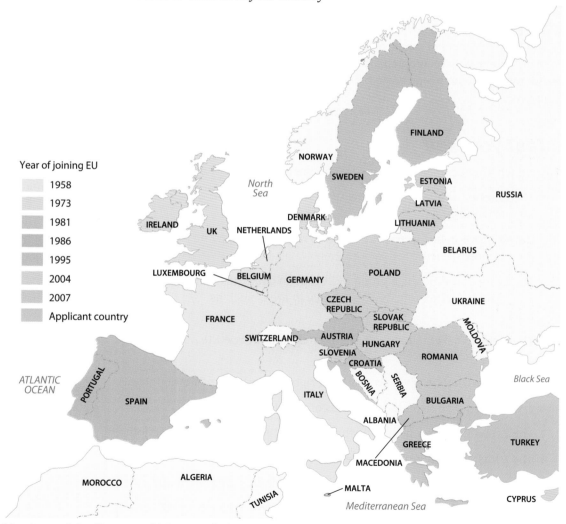

Year of joining EU

- 1958
- 1973
- 1981
- 1986
- 1995
- 2004
- 2007
- Applicant country

Members of the European Union as of 2010

- The EU has moved towards **harmonisation** of measurements, laws and currency. Most of the countries of the EU decided that it would be much easier for businesses and trade in general if all were using the same currency. This single currency, the euro, was introduced in 1999. The single currency has benefits to business (and overseas travellers), in that the charges and confusion that go with currency changes are avoided. It makes trade easier and smoother.
- Not all countries joined the euro, as it meant handing over control of some key decisions to the EU, such as the setting of interest rates. The UK has said it will not join until certain economic conditions have been met.

In a nutshell

* The EU is a powerful 'club' of nations with common goals and some common laws.
* There are advantages to joining the EU, and therefore countries wanting to join.
* The EU has made trade within its borders easier through a single system of measurements and free movement of goods and labour.
* Many countries have adopted the euro — the single currency of the EU.
* Adopting the euro brings some disadvantages as well as benefits, so not all countries have joined.

Test yourself

State whether each of the following statements is true or false.

1 The European Union passes laws and regulations which may affect businesses.

2 Harmonisation has been introduced to make trading with the EU more difficult.

3 The European Union is a group of European countries that have decided to act together, especially in areas such as trade.

4 The single market refers to the market within a single EU country.

5 The Social Chapter gives workers the right to work in any EU country.

6 The euro is used in all the countries of the EU.

7 The EU will not expand any further, as no other country wishes to join.

8 The UK is a member of the European Union.

9 The Maastricht Treaty lays down different rules for different member states.

10 The EU promises workers more say in businesses through worker councils.

Boost *your grade*

AO1 to AO2: you will not be asked to name the countries of the EU, or to say anything about its history. For AO2 marks, you should be able to discuss the benefits that the euro might bring in the context of the case study business.

Section test: The wider world

1 Fill in the missing words in the sentences below by choosing from the list given.
   (a) Globalisation means business and industry are more .... on each other.
   (b) Globalisation can mean that .... have a greater choice of products.
   (c) One of the strengths of many multinationals is their ....

   dependent   consumers   independent   employees   global brands

   (3 marks)

2 State whether each of the following statements about the European Union is true or false.
   (a) The EU will not expand any further, as no other country wishes to join.
   (b) Harmonisation has been introduced to make trading with the EU easier.
   (c) The euro is used in all the countries of the EU.
   (d) The single market refers to the market within a single EU country.
   (e) The Social Chapter gives workers the right to work in any EU country.   *(2 marks)*

3 Which TWO of the following are least likely to be 'external factors' affecting businesses?
   (a) Changes in taxation, (b) shareholder demands, (c) changes in interest rates,
   (d) increased dividends to pay, (e) changes in government spending.   *(2 marks)*

4 Changes in interest rates are decided by which ONE of the following?
   (a) The government, (b) the European Union, (c) the Bank of England,
   (d) high street banks, (e) the Financial Services Authority.   *(1 mark)*

5 An increase in VAT will have which ONE of the following effects?
   (a) An increase in sales from a product, (b) an increase in income,
   (c) an increase in the price of a product, (d) a decrease in income,
   (e) a decrease in the price of a product.   *(1 mark)*

6 If an American entrepreneur decided to open a branch of his Japanese restaurant chain in England, the restaurant would have to pay its UK employees in which currency?
   (a) US dollars, (b) European euros, (c) pounds sterling, (d) Canadian dollars,
   (e) Japanese yen.   *(1 mark)*

7 If a French tourist buys a holiday in Blackpool and pays €600 for it, and if the exchange rate is €1 = 90p, the holiday company will receive which of the following?
   (a) €540, (b) €600, (c) £540, (d) £600, (e) £666.   *(1 mark)*

8 If the exchange rate changed to €1 = 80p, what would be the price to pay now?
   (a) £540 or €600, (b) €600 or £480, (c) £540 or €540, (d) £600 or €600,
   (e) £540 or €480.   *(1 mark)*

9 The exchange rate change from €1 = 90p to €1 = 80p would be which THREE of the following? (a) Of benefit to the exporter, (b) of benefit to the importer, (c) a disadvantage to the exporter, (d) a disadvantage to the importer, (e) an advantage to the tourist. *(3 marks)*

The next three questions are based on the passage that follows. Read the passage and answer the questions.

Maserrari imports top-of-the-range sports cars from Italy. Many of its customers take out loans in order to buy the cars and Maserrari works with a credit company to provide these loans. Recently, one of the company's specialist car-cleaning machines broke down and it had to spend £10,000 on buying a new one from its American suppliers.

10 Which TWO of the following are the most likely effects on the business?
    (a) The business would not be affected because it had no savings.
    (b) The business would see a fall in demand.
    (c) The business would see its costs fall.
    (d) The business would see its sales slow down.
    (e) The business would see an increase in demand. *(2 marks)*

11 Calculate how much Maserrari would have to pay for its machine if the exchange rate between US dollars and pounds sterling was $1 = 65p. Show your working. *(2 marks)*

12 Which of the following might NOT be considered to be stakeholders in Maserrari?
    (a) its owners, the Maserrari family, (b) the American supplier from which it bought the machine, (c) Italian sports car manufacturers, (d) the government of Italy, (e) Italian pasta makers. *(1 mark)*

Total: 20 marks

Check your answers online at:
www.hodderplus.co.uk/philipallan

Practice exam

Case study

Material pre-released to candidates

Background

Zeitgeist plc is a worldwide business, specialising in sports shoes. Its head office is in Tinnerton, a new town about 15 miles from London, but it has operations all around the globe including the European Union, North and South America and the Far East. Zeitgeist operates a 'fair trade' policy. It tries to buy locally sourced materials and makes sure that some of the profits from its operations are ploughed back into the countries where it works.

Zeitgeist's five brands of sports shoes are produced in Fallowfell, a small town in the north of England. The shoes are sold in a very competitive market, amongst other famous brands.

The directors of Zeitgeist have to take decisions on the future of the company, based on data prepared for them by the various department heads in the company

Document 1: Managing director's report

John Young is managing director of Zeitgeist and explains, 'We have to walk a very fine line — we want to maintain quality, which means paying for top materials and processes, but we want to keep prices competitive. We also want to be fair to the communities where we work.' Zeitgeist is keen to aim for sustainable production as, globally, resource depletion increases. It also plans to use more renewable resources and alternative technologies.

Document 2: Finance director's report

Jodie Jones works as a financial director. In June of this year, she prepared the following cash-flow forecast for the last 6 months of the year. She is worried about the forecast growth in wages and advertising costs in December.

Cash-flow forecast for Zeitgeist plc for the last 6 months of the current year (£000)

	July	August	September	October	November	December
RECEIPTS						
Revenue from sales	900	800	750	650	800	1,600
PAYMENTS						
Wages and salaries	200	200	200	200	200	300
Materials	200	200	200	200	300	200
Power and maintenance	100	50	50	100	100	100
Rent	200	200	200	200	200	200
Transport	100	100	50	50	50	100

Advertising	150	100	100	50	100	300
Total payments	950	850	800	800	950	1,200
Net cash flow	−50	−50	−50	−150	−150	400
Opening balance	250	200	150	100	−50	−200
Closing balance	200	150	100	−50	−200	200

She also prepared these sales charts and comments.

Market share for Zeitgeist (blue) and Zike (red)

Jodie also reports that Zeitgeist's main competitor is Zike. The Zike Plus is a mid-range, all-purpose gym and running shoe priced at £49.99 a pair, which has taken 60% of this £10 million market due to recent heavy advertising campaigns. Despite planned increases in advertising, Jodie thinks Zeitgeist is unlikely to gain market share against this direct competitor unless it can cut price.

Document 3: Fallowfell management report

Production at the Fallowfell plant has been falling off in recent months. Staff at the factory say that the machinery has become old and breaks down too often. This has led to some quality issues, which our quality checks picked up too late to stop poor-quality shoes leaving the factory. This has affected demand. The recession has also had an effect across the entire industry.

Production could be back to last year's levels, with even lower costs, if we were to start a lean production system. I believe that we currently hold too much stock of raw materials and this could be reduced.

I also believe that we should move the job production of specialist shoes for individual athletes to nearer head office, so that the athletes can easily visit for fittings. We would also benefit from the publicity. Batch production of our more popular sizes could continue, under a just-in-time system, at Fallowfell.

The table gives figures for a typical week's production at Fallowfell (Triple Zees) and at Zike.

	Triple Zees	Zike Plus
Materials	£60,000	£75,000
Labour	£15,000	£10,000
Other overheads	£10,000	£7,500
Pairs produced	1,500	2,000
Price	£60	£50

Document 4: A recent email exchange

Email from Enterprise Africa to John Young

Dear John,

I am pleased to say that you will be able to secure an excellent deal with Enterprise Africa for production of Triple Zees. Low labour costs mean that we can keep fixed costs at £100,000 per year. Variable cost is £16 per shoe and we will be able to produce 6,000 pairs of shoes a year. Even with a 50% profit margin, the price you could charge would then be comparable with Zike.

Paul, Director, Enterprise Africa

Email from John Young to Enterprise Africa

Whilst I would like to take you up on your offer and move production to Africa, there are still some issues to iron out. If we closed our factory in Fallowfell, it would have huge social costs, as we are the only major employer in the area. Also, transporting shoes to our European and American markets would mean a much bigger carbon footprint. However, we have yet to make a decision and will be meeting later this month. I will be in touch once we have decided.

John, Managing Director, Zeitgeist plc

Question 1

(a) **Complete the following sentences using the terms given. Select the most appropriate term. Each term is only used once.**

(i) .... are carried by everyone in the community.

(ii) Increased production worldwide means that .... is an increasing problem.

(iii) Carbon dioxide emissions contribute to increased ....

(global warming)   (social costs)   (resource depletion)

(3 marks)

(b) **The following terms are used in the case study. Explain what each means.**
   (i)   carbon footprint
   (ii) sustainable production
   (iii) alternative technologies   *(6 marks)*

(c) **Suggest and explain THREE ways in which Zeitgeist could reduce its carbon footprint.**   *(6 marks)*

(d) **Suggest and explain TWO possible ethical issues for Zeitgeist if it moved production to Africa.**   *(6 marks)*

(e) **Evaluate why businesses like Zeitgeist aim to be environmentally responsible.**   *(6 marks)*

Total for question 1: 27 marks

Question 2

(a) **Which brand of mid-range sports shoe is currently the market leader?**   *(1 mark)*

(b) **Explain what has happened to the value of Zeitgeist's market share for Zeitgeist Triple Zees in this market over the past 6 months.**   *(5 marks)*

(c) **Explain why brand value is important to Zeitgeist.**   *(2 marks)*

(d) **The Fallowfell management report suggests that a just-in-time system might boost production.**
   (i) **Explain what is meant by 'just-in-time' (JIT) production.**
   (ii) **Analyse the possible advantages and disadvantages of JIT to Fallowfell and its workers.**   *(4 marks)*

(e) **At Fallowfell, batch production of shoes takes place. Explain the main features of this type of production.**   *(4 marks)*

(f) **Suggest and explain how a TQM system at Fallowfell could be better than quality checks on finished shoes.**   *(6 marks)*

(g) **Explain what effect the recession is having on Zeitgeist.**   *(6 marks)*

Total for question 2: 28 marks

Question 3

Jodie Jones has forecast the cash flow to the end of the current year.

(a) **In which month will Zeitgeist need to borrow the most?**   *(1 mark)*

(b) **Calculate the percentage change in wages between November and December.**   *(2 marks)*

(c) Jodie is worried about the forecast growth in wages and advertising costs in December. Explain the likely consequences of:
   (i)   reducing wage expenditure
   (ii) reducing advertising expenditure   *(4 marks)*

(d) Calculate the price that Zeitgeist could charge for its Triple Zees if it moved production to Enterprise Africa. Show your working.   *(8 marks)*

(e) Explain why this would be an appropriate and competitive price.   *(2 marks)*

(f) Net profit for a typical weekly production run of Zike Plus shoes has been calculated at £7,500.
   (i)   Calculate gross and net profit for Zeitgeist Triple Zees.   *(6 marks)*
   (ii) Explain which shoe is more profitable, assuming all production is sold. Give reasons for your answer, supported by figures from the case study and your own calculations.   *(8 marks)*
   (iii) Suggest ONE way in which Zeitgeist could become more competitive. Support your answer by referring to the case study.   *(4 marks)*

Total for question 3: 35 marks

Overall total: 90 marks

Check your answers online at:
www.hodderplus.co.uk/philipallan

Unit A291
Marketing and enterprise

Topic 44

Understanding the market

What the specification requires

You need to recognise that a successful business understands both its customers and the market in which it is operating. It can use market research to find out about both. It can also use business techniques such as market mapping to spot a gap in a market.

In brief

A market is anywhere that a buyer and seller come together to agree on a sale. In order to succeed, the business that is doing the selling needs to know as much as possible about the customer that is doing the buying. Most businesses succeed by either finding or creating a **gap in the market**. They do this by offering a product that is wanted, but which other businesses do not provide. They are likely to target particular parts of a market, called market segments.

Revision notes

- Making sure that the business knows what customers want, and then providing it, is essential to success. By providing products to the customers that want them, businesses are operating in a market.
- A market is anywhere that buyers and sellers come together to agree on the price for an amount of a product. This does not have to be a physical place: markets can take place via telephone or online. A product will be either a good or a service. **Goods** are things that can be touched; **services** are done for or to a customer.
- New businesses look for a gap in the market. A gap in the market is where a **demand** exists, but it is not being met. Businesses can map their market by listing its key features, then seeing where there are gaps.
- Some businesses are able to create a gap in the market by, for example, offering a completely new type of product.

- Market research may be collected from published sources (secondary) or be original (primary), such as interviews and questionnaires. One important source of such data is direct customer contact and feedback.
- Markets are often divided into segments. These can then be more easily targeted. Common ways of segmentation include age, geography, gender, hobbies and interests, and socioeconomic group — that is, the level of income and education enjoyed by a household.
- Market research may produce both quantitative and qualitative data. Quantitative data involve numbers and statistics. Qualitative data involve opinions, views and interpretations.

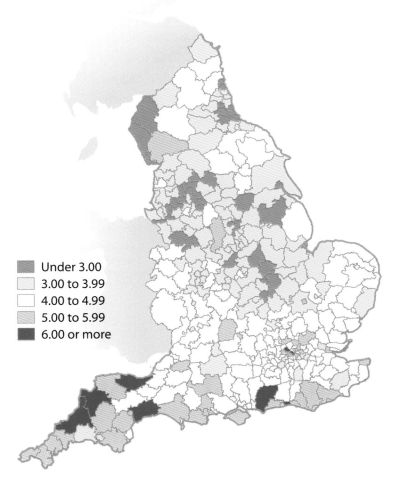

Under 3.00
3.00 to 3.99
4.00 to 4.99
5.00 to 5.99
6.00 or more

A map showing house prices in relation to income in England. For example, in the dark purple areas, a house will cost at least six times the average income. How can information like this help a business?

In a nutshell

* Businesses provide products to markets.
* To succeed, they need to find a gap in the market.
* This means analysing the market — both buyers and sellers.
* This can be achieved through market research.

Test yourself

In this section, the questions are designed to test your knowledge and understanding so that you can apply this to the controlled assessment.

Fill in the missing words using the list below. If you are feeling confident, cover the words and do the exercise from memory.

Businesses are set up in order to provide the .... that people need and want. Businesses sell and customers buy. This is called a .... Goods are things that can be touched as opposed to things done for or to a customer, called .... Markets are often divided into .... These can then be more easily targeted. Common ways of .... include age, geography, gender, hobbies and interests, and ....: that is, the level of income and education enjoyed by a household. Market research may produce both ...., involving numbers and statistics, and ...., involving opinions, views and interpretations.

AO1: to access Level 1 marks, you need to understand that the most important part of a business transaction is usually the customer. Being able to explain that keeping the customer happy is the basis for business success will give you AO1 marks in your controlled assessment.

(market) (products) (qualitative data) (quantitative data) (segmentation)

(segments) (services) (socio-economic group)

Topic 45

Marketing and market research

What the specification requires

Market research is the way in which businesses find out what customers want. Many methods of market research are either too expensive or too difficult for a small business to use. Larger businesses are often in a position to get better research.

In brief

Businesses need to collect information to help them to sell products to their customers. They need to know which group of customers might buy the product, how much they might be willing to spend, how often they will buy and what is attracting them to the product — why they want to buy. They can find out this information through various means, such as asking questions or looking at market data. With this information the business can decide not only what to sell, but also how to change a product or develop new products to attract customers.

Revision notes

- Market research involves the collection, collation, analysis and interpretation of data regarding a particular market.
- It may involve both **primary (field)** and **secondary (desk) research**.
- Primary research is information that has not been collected before; it is 'first-hand' information. Often the methods of collecting primary research make it expensive, but it can be targeted and focused to collect exactly the data required.
- Secondary research is research that has been previously published. There are very good sources of secondary data, such as government statistics, and many less reliable sources, such as the internet. Secondary research may be cheap (it may even be free — many government-collected statistics are available on the government website at **www.statistics.gov.uk**), but much of it will not fulfil the exact requirements of the business.

Advantages and disadvantages of different types of research

	Advantages	Disadvantages
Field research	■ Up to date ■ Targeted	■ Expensive ■ Time consuming ■ Large surveys needed for accuracy
Desk research	■ Cheap, even free ■ Easy to obtain	■ Out of date ■ Not exactly what is wanted ■ Some can be expensive

Questionnaires are one way for a business to gather information

- It is part of the marketing function to ensure that there is a good balance of primary and secondary sources. There is science behind asking the right questions or researching the right secondary information that often requires specialist researchers to produce the best results.
- Research may produce **quantitative** and **qualitative data** that have to be interpreted and analysed to be of use to a business.
- Quantitative data involve numbers and statistics, and will, for example, show trends.
- Qualitative data involve opinions, views and interpretations, so may give deeper insights, but will be harder to analyse. Small groups of people called 'focus groups' may be used to give opinions.
- Data are no use until they are interpreted. They then become 'information' which can be fed into the marketing mix.

In a nutshell

* The main types of research are field/primary and desk/secondary research.
* Field research is more reliable, but time consuming and expensive.
* Desk research is cheap — often free — but may be out of date or unreliable.
* Both quantitative and qualitative data are important.
* Data need to be interpreted to become information; this can then be used to support the marketing mix.

Test yourself

Choose the most appropriate answer from each of following alternatives.

1 Market research is usually divided into desk research and **(a)** open research, **(b)** field research, **(c)** closed research, **(d)** concentrated research.

2 The two main types of research are also known as **(a)** primary and tertiary, **(b)** secondary and tertiary, **(c)** primary and secondary, **(d)** outside and inside.

3 A small group asked for an opinion on a product is called **(a)** a focus group, **(b)** a delta group, **(c)** observation, **(d)** market data.

4 Company reports can be useful because they are easy to obtain and **(a)** free, **(b)** complicated, **(c)** online, **(d)** expensive.

5 The internet often provides free information. The main problem with this information is that it is not always **(a)** reliable, **(b)** easy to read, **(c)** searchable, **(d)** in English.

Boost *your grade*

AO2 to AO3: when presented with market research data, always ask yourself how valid it is. Look at the source and date. If you do not have raw data, but an opinion, this could be less reliable. For AO3 marks, use these arguments to support your analysis of data and as the reasons to support your judgements.

Topic 46

The marketing mix: product

What the specification requires

You should understand that, as a business grows, it may wish to expand its **product portfolio.** You should know that, as the demand for a good or service changes over time, there is a natural 'life cycle' and that businesses may try to extend this life cycle.

In brief

Businesses use different techniques at the launch phase of a product to persuade customers to try it. Product trial may involve special offers and promotions. Once a customer has tried (and likes) a product, the business then aims to encourage repeat purchase. This means using techniques such as loyalty cards to bring repeat business. Such techniques are used at different stages of the product life cycle. The Boston matrix can be used to analyse the product portfolio of a business.

Revision notes

- Businesses need to persuade customers to try a new product. They also want repeat sales. Different marketing techniques are used to achieve these two outcomes.
- The **product life cycle** (see the diagram and table overleaf) shows the usual stages through which a product passes. Like a person, a product is born, grows old, matures and eventually dies. Some life cycles are very short, or explosive. Others are very long or extended. The stage of the life cycle is important to a business. It shows it what sort of promotion or other changes might be needed to boost sales.
- The normal product life cycle is shown here. Each stage can be a short or long time. This will differ from product to product. The stages in the life cycle are:
  - development — during which no sales are made, but there are costs
  - launch — when the product is first offered for sale; costs can be high as the product needs to be advertised
  - growth — as sales grow, competitors will begin to think about bringing out rival products
  - maturity — many people have bought the product but there are now also competitors; promotion is still needed

> **Speak the language**
>
> **product portfolio** — the range of products offered by a business
>
> **product life cycle** — the way in which a product is born, grows and dies
>
> **extension strategy** — a way to make the life cycle longer

- decline — sales fall and the business must decide whether to try to extend the life cycle or let the product die
- Successful products can have their life cycle extended through product **extension strategies**. These may be changes to the product; finding new uses or applications; or additional promotion. These could add costs to the business but should also increase sales.

The product life cycle

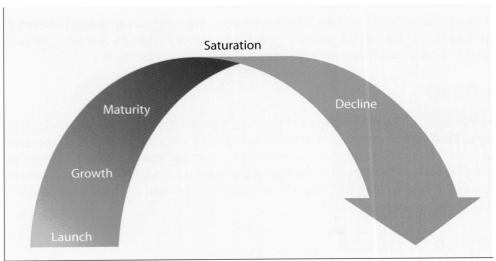

Stage	Description
1 Launch	The product is first brought out and introduced to the shops.
2 Growth	Sales grow as the product is advertised and becomes well known.
3 Maturity	Sales slow down. Most people have one, and now there are competing products
4 Saturation	Sales start to go down. Everybody's got one already. There are many competing products, which are often cheaper and better.
5 Decline	Sales fall further. The product is eventually withdrawn from the market.

In a nutshell

* Growing businesses can broaden their product portfolio.
* This helps them to compete.
* All products pass through a life cycle.
* Businesses use different ways to support the product at different stages.
* At launch, techniques to encourage product trial are used.

Test yourself

1 Describe 'launch' and the two stages that follow it in a product life cycle. *(3 marks)*

2 Explain why a particular marketing technique might be used in the first of these stages. *(3 marks)*

3 Suggest a product that is currently at this stage and describe how it might be marketed. *(4 marks)*

Boost your grade

AO2 to AO3: do not forget the importance of branding when a business creates a product range. Mentioning the term 'branding' as a way to 'differentiate' products clearly puts you at AO3 knowledge levels, so be sure to do this when writing up your controlled assessment.

Topic 47

The marketing mix: price

What the specification requires

Price is just one part of the marketing mix, but can be used to support business growth. Various pricing strategies can be used to gain market share and in order to compete more effectively. You should understand the factors which influence such pricing decisions.

In brief

Businesses can use effective **pricing techniques** to increase market share, to compete effectively and to further their growth. You should understand how such pricing decisions may be used, and how they are more or less effective according to the type of market in which the business operates and the degree of competition that it faces. You should also remember that businesses have to set prices so that they are competing and attracting customers. Some businesses are able to take a loss on certain products for a period, and this makes them more effective competitors in a market.

Revision notes

- The most common form of pricing is **cost-plus pricing**. This is where the business adds up the various costs of producing the product and then adds on a percentage for profit (called a **mark-up**).
- Most other methods of pricing are competitive, as they involve pricing in

Speak the language

pricing techniques — different ways to price a product

cost-plus pricing — totalling all the costs of producing a product, then adding a mark-up

mark-up — the percentage added to the costs to give the business a profit

A £5,000 wedding dress: how much is cost, how much is mark-up?

such a way that the business's products sell more than its competitors' products. Smaller businesses may not have access to these methods, whereas growing businesses will. Typical pricing strategies include:

- skimming — where a product (often new technology) can be sold at an opening high price to those who want to be first to own it
- penetration pricing — where a product can be sold at an opening low price to gain market share
- loss leaders — where a product is priced so low that it does not even cover its costs. This attracts buyers who realise the benefits of the product and continue to buy it. In retail terms a loss leader is usually a staple product (such as bread or milk), priced to attract customers into a shop so that they spend money on other products.

■ Pricing strategies such as these can only be used where a business has a dominant position in a market, such as having a new product, or where competitors cannot afford to match prices.

■ Some competitive pricing involves looking at what rivals are charging and matching this price. Businesses with a larger share of the market will be able to control this price, whereas smaller businesses must just accept the 'normal' price for a product, as set by the market.

In a nutshell

* Most businesses will price to cover costs.
* Growing businesses may have access to other pricing strategies, and therefore may be able to compete more effectively.
* Some of these are used to gain a market position.
* Others are used to compete more effectively.
* Many small businesses do not have this power, and must accept the market price.

Boost your grade **AO1 to AO2:** pricing techniques that you suggest must be suitable for both the product or brand and the market in which the business you are studying for your controlled assessment is operating. A bakery, for example, would be unlikely to find skimming useful, as this is usually linked to new technology products.

Test yourself

Match the term on the left with the correct definition on the right.

1	cost-plus pricing	setting price to cover the costs of a product
2	loss leaders	the percentage added to the cost-plus price for profit
3	mark-up	an opening low price to gain market share
4	penetration pricing	an opening high price for a new product
5	skimming	a price so low that it does not even cover its costs

Topic 48

The marketing mix: promotion

What the specification requires

You should know that promotional activities can be used to help and support brands as just one part of the marketing mix. Larger businesses can choose from a range of appropriate promotional methods. Businesses need to choose promotions carefully, taking into account the product itself, the market in which they are operating and the likely reaction of competitors.

In brief

Larger businesses may have more effective **promotional strategies**, first because they can afford them and second because, as they grow larger, they need to use them to reach wider markets. Methods that are not suitable for smaller businesses, such as television or national billboard campaigns, are more expensive but may also be more effective. Any method that is used will only be effective if it is appropriate to the product and effective in the market. The use of promotion in a competitive market may be countered by other businesses increasing their own levels of promotion.

Industrial and other goods are promoted through trade fairs

Larger businesses can afford to sponser events such as Formula 1 racing

Revision notes

- Growing businesses are able to afford a much greater range of promotional strategies than small businesses.
- Advertising is publicity for a product that is paid for directly; it is called **above-the-line** expenditure. Advertising is used to promote products through broadcast and print media, such as television, radio, posters, magazines, leaflets and point-of-sale material. Larger businesses can afford to use outlets such as television. Such outlets tend to be more effective as they reach a wider audience. However, they are also more expensive.
- Sales promotion is called **below-the-line** expenditure. Growing businesses can use sales promotion techniques such as loss leaders (see page 130), special offers (such as buy one, get one free), competitions, money-off coupons, free samples and trials, joint promotions with other businesses (e.g. washing powders recommended by washing machine manufacturers) and loyalty cards. Growing businesses may also be able to market and sell directly to the customer, through websites or catalogues, for example. This is called direct marketing.

- Sponsorship means that the product will be associated with a certain event or sport, or what is good about the event — a marathon race could promote fitness, for instance. Larger businesses can afford to sponsor larger and more widely recognised teams, events or organisations.
- The business should choose the promotional mix that is going to be most effective in its target market. This depends on the nature of the market (e.g. is the producer a market leader; does it have power in the market?), the type of product (e.g. is it essential or easily substituted?), and how competitors react to increased promotion.

Speak the language

promotional strategies — any method designed to increase awareness and sales of a product

above-the-line — directly paid-for advertising

below-the-line — promotions that increase sales, but are not advertising

In a nutshell

* Bigger businesses can use a greater range of promotional strategies.
* They can afford sales promotions.
* They can use national advertising media.
* They can sponsor big and widely recognised events.

Boost your grade

AO3: for AO3 marks, you should be able to argue for and against promotion and then form a judgement. The main case for promotion is that it informs — without it customers would not know what was on offer and would therefore not be able to make a choice. The case against is that it is an unnecessary cost, which is passed on to the consumer. Spend your time in the controlled assessments making judgements like this, rather than doing low-level work such as designing advertisements.

Test yourself

Fill in the missing words using the list below. If you are feeling confident, cover the words and do the exercise from memory.

A business should choose the .... that is going to be most effective in its .... This depends on the nature of the ...., the type of .... and how .... react to increased promotion. Larger businesses can afford better ...., such as .... like competitions and joint .... with other businesses. They can also sell directly to customers through .... They can afford .... of well-known teams or events.

competitors   joint promotions   market   product   promotional mix

promotional techniques   sales promotions   sponsorship   target market   websites

Topic 49

The marketing mix: place

What the specification requires

You should understand that, as a business succeeds, it may need to access a wider customer base. To do so may mean that it needs to broaden the distribution channels it already has, or add new channels to reach more potential customers. You should be able to match appropriate sales outlet and distribution channels, and recognise that this is just one part of the marketing mix.

In brief

A growing business will need to access more customers, so may need more, or better, distribution channels. Most businesses sell to wholesalers or retailers, but could also extend their reach by selling directly to customers. This could be via direct sales, telephone sales or the internet. The choice of distribution channel will be affected by the nature of the product, the customers and the market in which the business operates.

Raw material producer → Manufacturer → Wholesaler → Retailer → Consumer

A traditional long chain of distribution

Revision notes

- **Place** refers to where a product is sold and how the product gets there. Growing businesses may need to choose different locations at which to sell and **channels of distribution** to access a larger customer base. The main channels used by businesses are:
  - Retail outlets, ranging from small corner shops to hypermarkets and department stores. Many still specialise in a particular product, while others offer a general range. Some major retailers will not offer shelf space to more than the brand leader and their own brand. This can be a problem for products that are popular but not leaders.
  - Wholesalers. These allow the business to sell bulk stock, making room for new production. However, wholesalers will not pay as high a price for products as either retailers or consumers.

> **Speak the language**
>
> **place** — both sales location and how goods arrive there
>
> **channels of distribution** — ways to deliver goods to customers, or to where customers can buy them
>
> **cold call** — a sales telephone call made with no previous contact with the customer

Transport at each stage of the chain adds to costs

- Telesales. This is where products are sold directly to consumers via a telephone call. Often telesales are done to sell products additional to those already owned (e.g. additional insurance or a new banking service). **Cold calls** do not tend to be very effective.
- Mail order. Here a business provides a catalogue or advertises in a newspaper or magazine. Such direct sales are only possible where delivery costs are not a major factor.
■ With internet sales, products are delivered to buyers. The product range can be viewed via a website. Websites open up worldwide markets but, again, delivery costs may be a major factor.
■ To judge whether or not a distribution channel is appropriate, a business needs to consider its own needs and those of its customers. Important factors for the business are cost, availability and profit margins. Important factors for customers are convenience, cost and reliability.

In a nutshell

* Growing businesses may need to access more customers.
* To do this, they may need more distribution channels.
* This could mean more traditional channels, such as retailers.
* It may mean more modern channels, such as the internet.

Test yourself

State whether each of the following statements is true or false.

1 Delivery costs are a major factor in internet selling.

2 For customers, the important factors of distribution are cost, availability and profit margins.

3 Services are easy to sell and deliver via distance selling.

4 Important factors for customers relating to distribution are convenience, cost and reliability.

5 Some goods are not suitable for online sales.

6 A growing business will need wider methods of distribution.

7 The way goods are distributed is called a channel.

8 A cold call is used to follow up a sales lead.

9 Place refers just to the place where goods are sold.

10 The internet helps retailers reach more customers.

AO2 to AO3: you should try to show the depth of your understanding by using recent examples linked to your controlled assessment business. For example, many questions on distribution will be talking about online sales and how these have changed the market. You will gain AO3 marks by using this in your reasoning.

Topic 50

The marketing mix: e-commerce

What the specification requires

You should be able to explain the importance of e-commerce and internet selling activities to a business. You should be able to consider the advantages and disadvantages of e-commerce and how this fits within an overall marketing framework for a business.

In brief

E-commerce has become a major way for businesses to trade. The term 'e-commerce' refers to buying and selling goods or services over the internet. Usually it involves a website and a means of ordering and paying electronically. Businesses either operate as pure 'dotcom' companies (Dell is an example), with no physical shops or other outlets, or with a combination of websites and high street premises (Tesco is an example).

Revision notes

- Businesses need to learn to take advantage of new technologies to keep costs low. For instance, broadband is now widely available, while VOIP (Voice Over Internet Protocol) connections are allowing phone calls, even international ones, to be made for free.
- For the small and medium-sized business, there are two main possibilities for expansion on the internet. These are **B2C** and **B2B** — business to consumer, and business to business. While the rate of growth has slowed down in both sectors, growth is still taking place. In addition, there is a third growing market in business to government, or **B2G**.
- Businesses cannot just put up a website and hope customers will come calling. They need to advertise it (using traditional media) and make sure that it is registered on **search engines**. The key differences between a good and a poor website are shown in the table.

Speak the language

B2C — selling from business to consumer

B2B - selling from business to business

B2G - selling from business to government

search engines — programs that search for websites using key words

Good website	Bad website
■ Customers can find it easily	■ Difficult to find
■ Customers can find their way around (navigate) easily	■ Difficult to read (because of choice of fonts or an over-complex page design)
■ Easy to read	■ Not secure
■ Safe and secure	■ Hard to navigate
■ Reliable	

Personalised Home | Sign in

Web   Images   Groups   News   Froogle   **more »**

Google Search   I'm Feeling Lucky

Advanced Search
Preferences
Language Tools

Search: ⦿ the web ○ pages from the UK

Advertising Programmes - Business Solutions - About Google - Go to Google.com

©2006 Google

Google is one of the most popular search engines

- Websites are governed by the same consumer laws as shops. Goods and services must still be 'as described' and 'fit for purpose', and customers must be able to get their money back if they are not. The UK government has drawn up special distance selling regulations for websites and others that sell 'remotely' — that is, over the phone, or via catalogues.
- There is still a lot of growth to go. There are now over a billion users of the internet worldwide. This still represents only around a sixth of the world's population, with the biggest growth markets being in Asia (especially China) and Africa.

In a nutshell

* E-commerce has become a major way for businesses to trade.
* The term refers to buying and selling goods or services over the internet.
* Businesses need to take advantage of new technologies to keep costs low.
* Businesses need to advertise websites and register with search engines.
* Websites are governed by the same consumer laws as shops.
* There is still a lot of internet growth to go.

Boost your grade **AO1 to AO2:** as one way to encourage small businesses, there is government help in the form of both advice and information. Research the UK government assistance that is available by visiting **www.businesslink.gov.uk**.

Test yourself

Explain how the business that you have chosen to investigate could benefit from the use of e-commerce.

(5 marks)

Section test: Controlled assessment

1. Which of the following is NOT a main source for desk research? **(a)** Books, **(b)** newspapers and journals, **(c)** questionnaires, **(d)** internet.

2. Which of the following is NOT a feature of field research?
   - **(a)** It is targeted.
   - **(b)** It is up to date.
   - **(c)** It is inexpensive.
   - **(d)** It is time consuming.

3. Which of the following is NOT a recognised route for e-commerce trading?
   (a) B2B, **(b)** B2C, **(c)** B2G, **(d)** G2G.

4. A narrow product mix means that **(a)** the business makes products and services, **(b)** the business makes a range of goods, **(c)** the business concentrates on a few products, **(d)** the business sells a range of services.

5. Creating a memorable name or image for a product is called **(a)** product recognition, **(b)** targeted advertising, **(c)** product mixing, **(d)** branding.

6. Where a product fails to live up to expectations, its life cycle is said to be **(a)** shortened, **(b)** extended, **(c)** aborted, **(d)** saturated.

7. Which of the following is NOT a recognised part of a product life cycle? **(a)** Development, **(b)** maturity, **(c)** decline, **(d)** popularity.

8. Cost-plus pricing is calculated as **(a)** fixed cost plus variable cost, **(b)** cost plus mark-up, **(c)** start-up cost plus variable cost, **(d)** revenue minus costs.

9. Below-the-line promotion is **(a)** paid-for advertising, **(b)** not-paid-for advertising, **(c)** not directly paid-for advertising, **(d)** not very effective advertising.

10. The traditional channel of distribution involving manufacturers, wholesalers and retailers is called **(a)** short chain, **(b)** long chain, **(c)** complex distribution, **(d)** intermediate distribution.

Check your answers online at:
www.hodderplus.co.uk/philipallan

Speak the language index